Praise for *Enso House*

"What a unique and richly inspiring book—a fascinating and heartwarming adventure into realms not usually explored: What is it like to be dying? What is it like to be up front and close to that experience, caring for someone in that condition? Some surprising insights...reading it one finds oneself humbled and unexpectedly opened in deeply moving ways."

—Ven. Mitra Bishop, Abbot, Mountain Gate Zen Temple and Spiritual Director, Hidden Valley Zen Center

"This marvelous book is a story of courage and vision, as a small group of people, following the inspiration of a remarkable Zen teacher, establishes a 'house' where dying people can be cared for in a very special way. Reading this book, I am reminded of how great is the human spirit, how wide and deep the human heart."

—Joan Halifax, Founding Abbot, Upaya Zen Center, and author of *Being with Dying: Cultivating Compassion and Fearlessness in the Presence of Death*

Enso House

Caring for Each Other at the End of Life

David Daiku Trowbridge

Abiding Nowhere Press
Greenbank, Washington

ISBN 978-0-9854967-0-8

Library of Congress Control Number: 2013900586

Printed in the United States of America

To all who have volunteered their skills, talents, and time in the service of Enso House. May our community thrive for a thousand years.

The Task

When each of your days
Is sacred to you,

When each one of your hours
Is sacred to you,

When every instant
Is sacred to you,

When the earth and you,
And space with you,
Bear the sacred
All the length of your days,

Then you will be
In the fields of glory.

—Guillevic[1]

Table of Contents

Preface ix

Introduction xiii

My Aging Father 3

Opportunities Merge 5

Vision of a Roshi 27

Gift of Land 41

Commitment 61

Volunteers and Benefactors 77

The Practice of Caregiving 97

Guests as Teachers 109

Death with Dignity 161

Zen Training and Death 173

My Father's Final Days 187

Epilogue: Lessons Learned 215

Afterword by Shodo Harada Roshi 221

Acknowledgments 229

Notes 235

About the Author 237

PREFACE

I am an unlikely writer on the subject of end-of-life care. My academic training was in physics, and I worked in the field of software development. Having inherited my father's love of science, I expected to become a scientist or a science teacher. The constant theme of my education invariably tended to scientific study. But a number of forces conspired to redirect my life toward more intangible things and provide some transformative opportunities.

In my early twenties, I was unexpectedly introduced to the life and teaching of Siddhartha Gautama, which gave me a new perspective. I see this as the turning point that led me to Zen Buddhism and eventually hospice care. I was determined to experience a side of life that cannot be framed in objective terms. In the end, we each lose everything we hold most dear: our friends, our family, our possessions, our health, our fame, even our sense of who we are. The establishment of Enso House gave me an opportunity for new kinds of subjective experience. I think spiritual practice gradually led to a softening of my views about the primacy of science. I still have the same deep love of keen observation, rational thought and evidence, and have maintained an avocation in science. But I have also developed an appreciation for experience that lies outside of the scientific worldview.

This book begins with my story of how, as a graduate student in physics, I took an extended detour into other realms—both geographic and spiritual. The first five chapters are devoted to the stories of the people whose lives became intertwined and eventually led to the formation of Enso House.

Beginning with our very first guest, it was clear that Enso House would be a nexus for amazing stories, which are told in the middle chapters of the book. I gathered stories by interviewing various people connected with Enso House—those involved in its formation, staff members, caregivers, volunteers, and family members of guests. Our experiences and reflections over the years about Enso House plus my own experience with my father's passing constitute the final chapters of the book.

Writing this book was a collaborative process. I recorded and transcribed forty individual interviews. Using the transcripts I wrote an initial draft of each story, and then shared it with the person(s) I had interviewed. Together, we made additions, deletions and changes for accuracy, clarity and brevity. Direct quotes were edited, making sure we were keeping true to the intended meaning. Members of my writing group provided additional editorial suggestions. Family members and friends of Enso House guests were consulted and I obtained permission to publish their stories. This is a work of nonfiction and no pseudonyms have been used. I have tried to verify facts using multiple sources, but that was not always possible. Surely there are still errors in the book; if I am made aware of them, I will try to make corrections, if possible.

The number of guests whose stories are told here is a small sample of the seventy guests who have come to Enso House. Every death is unique and there is far more to tell than can be captured between the covers of a book. While not every person I interviewed has been quoted directly, everyone I talked with has informed the book.

Many of the people mentioned in this book have *dharma* names—names given to them by their Buddhist teacher in accordance with their practice. I have tried to indicate both dharma names and given names to help the reader navigate stories in which name usage changes over time and circumstance.

For reasons I may never understand, Enso House continues to attract people who want to give of themselves, to volunteer their time and apply their talents. Those who have been close to Enso House have discovered a way of being with dying people that can serve as an alternative to the way many people die today. At a time in America when we are reexamining what it means to take care of each other and ensure that everyone who needs care can find it, Enso House serves as an exemplary model.

This book is my way of expressing gratitude for these discoveries.

David Daiku Trowbridge
Greenbank, Washington
January, 2013

INTRODUCTION

E very once in a while, a group of people, recognizing a need that is self-evident, declares a mission and starts a project that thrives naturally in the community where it is born. This is the story of one such project.

Enso House, a home on Whidbey Island in the Pacific Northwest, takes as its sole purpose providing care for people at the end of life. Inspired by the practice of compassion and cultivated by spiritual training, the all-volunteer staff of Enso House serves individuals from Whidbey Island and neighboring communities. This book tells some of the stories of those people whose paths have intersected and led to the creation of this special place; and it tells the stories of those whose loved ones have passed away at Enso House. It describes the unique symbiotic relationship that has developed between a monastery, a home for the dying, and the community that nurtures both.

The vision for Enso House originated with the Zen Buddhist teacher Shodo Harada Roshi. He was looking for an opportunity to serve the Whidbey Island community where he had established a training monastery. In his vision, Enso House would have two purposes: to serve the needs of families seeking help caring for their loved ones as they approached the end of life and to provide a training ground for Zen students who wanted to experience the dying process up close.

For my wife, Cynthia, and for me, the creation of Enso House has been one of the most important and meaningful events of our life together. This act of giving and letting go connected us to something much bigger than ourselves. Cynthia knew instantly and intuitively that purchasing the land and making the home available for hospice care was the right thing to do. It generally takes me much longer to figure out things like this. But we have both been immensely grateful for the opportunity to walk this path.

Enso House

MY AGING FATHER

I'm not afraid of dying; I just don't want to be there when it happens.

—*Spike Milligan*[2]

"The first word is *kite*. The second word is *Lucille*. The third word...the third word...the third word I can't remember." My ninety-one-year-old father, Leslie, is struggling to tell us his progress on the book he is determined to write. His words are slurred, and his voice is raspy. He strains to find the words to describe his childhood memories of building a kite with his brother Bob, and about the tigers and bears that haunted the woods along the way to school that their older classmate, Lucille, had warned them about.

My father knows that he has precious little time left to tell his stories, and he doesn't have time for the interruptions to check his vital signs—his heart rate, blood pressure, and blood oxygen content. His single goal is to write another book before he dies, and he wants to make this clear to his therapist: he really cannot afford to take so much time to lift weights, pedal the stationary bicycle, and repeatedly practice lifting himself up from his chair to his walker.

In his writing projects, Dad has been an avid computer user for thirty years, but his skills are slipping. Blind in one eye and shaky in his hands, he has returned to using his fifty-year-old Smith Corona Electra 12 typewriter. Now, even inserting a sheet of paper in the typewriter is a challenge for him. So the typewriter sits idle on the table in his darkened room at his rehab facility, holding a misaligned sheet of paper with the words "kite Lucille."

My father had a lifelong devotion to science education and played a key role in an international movement to improve science teaching and learning. He had served as President of the National Science Teachers Association, was the author of sixteen books, and mentored hundreds of students in many countries. Now he was struggling to write a simple sentence—compelled to tell his story before he died. How much time did he have left?

And how much time do I have left to tell my story? How can I convey my amazement with the confluence of circumstances that brought me to the people I love? How can I describe events that seem to border on the miraculous?

OPPORTUNITIES MERGE

Two roads diverged in a wood, and I—
I took the one less traveled by,
And that has made all the difference.

—*Robert Frost*[3]

A s a first-year graduate student in Physics at the University of Washington in 1969–70, I was not doing very well academically—mainly because I was preoccupied with the prospect of being drafted and sent to Vietnam. I was caught up in the politics of the Vietnam War. Draft deferments for graduate students had ended, and the Selective Service had set up a lottery based on birth date. My friends were leaving the country to live in Canada or going to great lengths to disqualify themselves from military service. Some of my friends went on starvation diets to lose weight. Others discovered imaginative ways to express mental illness, which they had documented by sympathetic psychiatrists. My birth date, August 31, came up as number eleven in the lottery system, so I was looking at being drafted any day. At that time, I learned that it was possible to postpone induction to the military by joining the Peace Corps. I went to the local Peace Corps recruiting office and filled out an application. Two weeks later, I received an invitation to join a group of twenty other volunteers to teach math and science in villages in Nepal.

I may have heard the name of the country before, but I knew next to nothing about it. I headed straight to the Suzzalo library at the University of Washington. *Nepal.* Wow—the highest mountains in the world! Remote mountain valleys home to over a dozen languages in a country only five hundred miles from end to end! Muslims, Hindus, and Buddhists all living in harmony! Without a moment's hesitation, I accepted the invitation.

The two-month training in Davis, California, was intense and invigorating. We were immersed in language training eight hours a day. We were given historical and cultural enrichment, and took classes in teacher training. In January 1971, we left for Nepal, where I began my teaching assignment at Buddha Padma high School, a village school in Kapilvastu, Nepal.

My village, Taulihawa, was only about a mile from Tilaurakot, the site where in 1962 archeologists had discovered evidence for civilization dating back to the time of the Buddha[4]. This was the place where Siddhartha Gautama grew up in the palace of his father, Suddhodana, in the sixth century BCE. This was where, at age twenty-nine, he left his wife and family, and set out on a quest for liberation, eventually becoming known as the Buddha, or The Awakened One. I began looking for books about Buddhism and reading about the life of the Buddha.

In the autumn of 1971, an archeological team from Rissho University in Japan came to Tilaurakot to excavate the site. One day, the director of the project gave me a tour of the site and showed me many of the artifacts they had uncovered: coins, pottery, and terracotta figurines. He explained that his team had identified twelve distinct occupations at this site, evidenced by layers of soil that reached to a depth of about ten feet. The lowest layer they had uncovered dated to the time of the Buddha. As I walked on the scraped clay surface, I marveled at the fact that I could be walking on the same floor the Buddha had walked on twenty-five hundred years before.

In my reading, I soon came across Phillip Kapleau's book *The Three Pillars of Zen*[5]. Emphasizing Zen as a practical way of living and spiritual training, rather than as a philosophy, it caught my attention.

At the end of my second year of service, I decided to extend my stay for a third year. The Peace Corps granted extendees a roundtrip ticket to the United States to visit family. I thought this would be a good opportunity to swing by Japan and see what I could find out about Zen. So after spending Christmas with my parents in Colorado, I headed back to Nepal in January 1973, with a weeklong stopover in Japan.

I arrived in Tokyo with no leads as to where to go or how to find out anything about Zen. I came across a directory, similar to a Yellow Pages phone book, and looked up *Zen Buddhist Temples*. I found a Zen temple not far away and went to visit, craning my neck on a crowded bus, trying to match the occasional street name with the address I had written on a slip of paper.

At the temple, a congenial monk greeted me and gave me a brief introduction to their programs. They offered classes in tea ceremony and flower arranging. He gave me the schedule. I thanked him but explained that I was looking for a place that would help me with my personal Zen practice. He immediately knew what I was talking about and exclaimed, "Oh, you must see Mumon Yamada Roshi in Kobe." I had never heard of Mumon Yamada, but I took down the address and phone number for the temple Shofukuji and booked a train ticket to Kobe.

When I arrived in Kobe, I spent the night at a *ryokan*, a traditional Japanese inn. That evening I called the number for Shofukuji. A monk who spoke some English answered. I told him I hoped to visit the temple, and we agreed that I would show up around eight the next morning.

I took a train to the temple and arrived just before eight o'clock. I knocked on the temple gate but got no answer. I waited. Then I knocked again—still no answer. I waited patiently. After some twenty minutes, I knocked a third time—to no avail. I then remembered reading a story about a monk who arrived at a Zen monastery hoping to be admitted, but was refused initially. He needed to be exceptionally persistent before he was admitted. I decided that I too could be persistent, so I waited patiently.

Occasionally I heard sounds within the temple grounds, so I knew there were people inside. Four hours passed before a monk finally came out and greeted me. He said I should meet a couple of Americans who were living as monks in the monastery. Before long, two young men came out and introduced themselves: Thomas Kirchner (Yuho) and Dennis Tucker (Daikatsu). It turned out that Dennis was also a graduate of my alma mater, Reed College. He had graduated a couple of years after me. He had won a Watson Scholarship, a prestigious award worth about ten thousand dollars that could be used by the recipient to do whatever he liked. Dennis chose to live as a monk at a Zen monastery in Japan, and he found Shofukuji, one of the few Buddhist training monasteries that accepted foreigners.

Tom and Dennis explained they had just finished a *sesshin*, a seven-day intensive meditation retreat, and they wanted to go out and grab a couple of burgers. That caught me by surprise, but I said, "Sure, let's go." We went out to have hamburgers for lunch.

I stayed the night at the monastery and arranged to have tea with the Roshi the next day. I joined the monks for their evening meal, which involved wolfing down rice and vegetables from lacquered bowls, then washing the bowls with tea water and drinking the slurry. My bowls clattered and bits of rice on the table gave evidence of where I'd sat.

The next day I went in to have tea with Yamada Roshi. He spoke some English, so I didn't need a translator. I told him, "I don't know much, but one thing I do know is that sometimes I am a little more sane and sometimes a little less sane."

Yamada Roshi paused for a moment, stroked his beard, and then replied,

"Americans are very honest."

This brief exchange had a powerful effect on me. It validated my practice. I interpreted his response as a confirmation that I was on the right track—I was doing what I needed to do. In hindsight, this was a milestone and a turning point in my life. I found a commitment to Zen practice that has sustained me ever since.

I was soon leaving Japan, off to Nepal, returning to my village in Taulihawa. It would be nearly three decades before I saw Thomas Kirchner and Dennis Tucker again.

For my third year in Nepal, I had requested permission to move out of the home of the headmaster's family where I had stayed the first two years and into a place of my own. Living with an extended family was a great opportunity for interacting with people and developing fluency in the Nepali language, but it limited the amount of time I could commit to quiet meditation.

Gopal Singh, the headmaster, arranged for me to live on the upper floor of a new building being used to store grain below. I had two rooms: one served as a kitchen and bedroom; the other I set up as a meditation room. The apartment was about half a mile east of town, in a quiet location next to a mango grove. I continued my job as a science and math teacher at Buddha Padma High School. Having become more comfortable with Nepali, and having established some real friendships, my third year was my best year—most productive, most fun, most memorable, and above all, a unique opportunity to establish a regular sitting practice.

I remember trying to sit cross-legged in my meditation room. There wasn't any glass in the windows—just steel bars for security—so mosquitoes were free to come and go as they pleased. I rigged up a tent of mosquito netting around my sitting cushions, but I still had to be careful to squeeze into and out of the tent without letting mosquitoes in. At the beginning, I could keep my legs crossed for no more than five minutes. Through yoga stretching and persistence, I gradually increased the time that was bearable to about thirty minutes. To this day, I consider my ability to sit in half lotus one of my most valuable capabilities. It means that I always have a means of returning to a quiet, safe, dependable "home" whenever my mind is too excited, stressed, or somnolent.

In the summer of 1973, I took the train to Hyderabad, India, where I attended my first formal meditation retreat. It was led by S.N. Goenka in the Vipassana tradition, which emphasized awareness of the breath and paying close attention to body sensations. Maintaining silence for ten days was an option, which I chose; I only spoke when asking questions of Goenka or describing my practice to him. It made me realize how distracting talk can be, but also how important carefully chosen words can be.

After completing my three-year assignment in the Peace Corps, I returned to Seattle to continue my graduate studies. I felt committed to continue my sitting practice and learned of a Zen meditation group led by Wes Borden, a professor in the Chemistry Department at the University of Washington.

In the spring of 1974, I called Wes one evening to inquire about joining his sitting group. Wes sounded pleased to hear from me. He mentioned that another person, a young woman who had been coming to his home for weekly zazen, would be departing for Europe shortly, so my call was opportune in that I would be able to take her place in the zendo. I made a habit of joining the group on Thursday evenings for zazen, but it would be five years before I actually met the person on whose cushion I was sitting—and discovered my soul mate.

Cynthia Powell would become my partner in life as well as the energetic force behind our involvement with Enso house. Cynthia's background in end-of-life care and her intuitive sense of its importance would validate my own tentative intuitions.

———————⊙·⊙·⊙———————

Cynthia left Seattle and Wes' meditation group in 1974 to return to traveling. Having spent several years in Europe after college, she returned to the Continent intending to travel overland to India and Nepal. On the way, she made a little detour. She had a Scottish friend who took her to the Isle of Skye, a place she found completely captivating. She ended up staying on the island for five years, where she co-owned a crafts shop and waitressed at seasonal hotels. The winters were long and dark—at latitude 57° N, the sun is up for a mere seven to eight hours a day. Cynthia and her friends passed the time listening to BBC radio.

Cynthia remembers a program about end-of-life care featuring Cecily Saunders, the person who was responsible for starting the hospice movement in Britain. She says, "I was immediately drawn to that work, and I felt that I wanted to do hospice nursing. It was just a very strong desire."

While living in Skye, Cynthia received some disturbing news about her father: he had been suffering from headaches and occasional seizures, and doctors had discovered a large brain tumor. A surgeon was able to remove most of the tumor, but not all of it. They gave him six to twelve months to live. Cynthia knew she needed to leave Skye and return to the States immediately.

Cynthia quickly booked a flight and spent several months near her family. Her father had several heavy doses of radiation, which proved effective, giving him twelve more years. Cynthia felt this was a genuine wakeup call to her about life and death, a call to learn more about end-of-life care.

She took a sociology course, *Death and Dying*, at Seattle Central Community College. Later, she worked as a volunteer in a hospice at Providence Hospital. It was 1980, and this was the first hospice program in Seattle. Cynthia was in the first volunteer group trained at Providence Hospital on Cherry Hill, and she remembers it as a wonderful group to work with. The hospice program was started by a nurse and supported by physicians. Volunteers had many hours of comprehensive training, and after finishing the training program they were each assigned a patient. Some patients were in the hospital, and some were at home. Regardless, volunteers stayed with them until they died.

Cynthia remembers some of the patients she worked with.

"I remember a woman, probably in her sixties, close to my own mother's age. She had challenging relationships with her two daughters. For some reason, her daughters weren't able to touch her. She really wanted to be touched, but couldn't get it from her daughters. I discovered that I could step in and do that for them.

"Each person I worked with really valued the connection with hospice volunteers. They were each lonely in the big city of Seattle, many with no family there."

In coping with her father's illness and processing the emotions arising from being with others who were dying, Cynthia found it helpful to set aside time to just sit quietly. She was aware of meditation practices used in various spiritual traditions and began trying it herself. Here she describes her own experience with meditation.

"In my early twenties, I started doing some sitting, and it just made sense, quietly sitting in meditation; just quieting the mind seemed like the most pure spiritual experience. It just felt so comfortable. I had read *The Three Pillars of Zen*, but I didn't do a whole lot of reading because I didn't want to get caught up in all the dogma. The practice of just sitting was where it was at for me.

"I'm still at the same place now of feeling more drawn to sitting than getting caught up in all the texts and myths of Buddhism. What I do know is that being still is important."

Virtues of sitting meditation were discovered by many young people in the early seventies. One such person was Kurt Hoelting of Seattle whom we didn't meet until years later. Kurt was a halibut fisherman, deeply concerned with environmental stewardship, who came to Whidbey Island to further these pursuits. He came to meditation practice seeking an intelligent response to the environmental degradation and loss of wilderness he saw happening in the world. Pursuing the parallel endeavors of spiritual practice and environmental activism, he spent the winter of 1974 living in a small homestead cottage on Wahl Road on south Whidbey Island. Kurt would later develop a deeper connection with that property when his father became a guest at Enso House.

⎯⎯◉◉◉⎯⎯

In 1974, I was back in graduate school studying physics at the University of Washington. The War in Vietnam was over, and the draft had ended. In the Physics Department, a new group was forming that focused on research into student learning. I had found my science teaching experience in Nepal very rewarding, so I decided to join that group and make physics education the focus of my PhD dissertation.

I completed my PhD in 1979 and then accepted a postdoctoral appointment at the university. Another group in the Health Sciences Department at the university had just won a grant to support programs that helped students from academically disadvantaged backgrounds enter careers in the health sciences. The purpose of the grant was to increase enrollment of minority students in premed courses.

Cynthia Powell was the administrative assistant for the project. The principal investigator contacted the Physics Education Group about possible collaboration. They were looking for someone who might like to explore the possibilities of incorporating microcomputers into the laboratories. Their grant included some money for purchasing a few of the newly released Apple II computers.

My supervisor in the Physics Education Group suggested that I might be interested in exploring possible applications of these computers in science instruction. I was delighted to hear of this new opportunity and eager to begin. As administrative assistant, Cynthia was the contact person. I called her up and arranged to go over to her office to discuss the project.

Of course, I was excited about the prospect of getting a computer, but when I met Cynthia, I discovered other excitements. She had a strong Scottish accent, which I found delightfully attractive. Her face was bright, and she had a cheerful disposition. We talked and talked about her recent travels in Scotland and mine in Nepal. It was really exciting discovering all the things we had in common and how close our values and perspectives dovetailed—not the same, but complementary.

Small talk is not my strong suit, but I lingered in her office well beyond what was required to make arrangements for receiving the computer. I paced back and forth in front of her desk, telling her about myself and my experiences in Nepal. We had a lot to talk about and discovered that we shared an interest in Buddhism.

Part of Cynthia's responsibility was to make sure that the university's inventory stickers were attached to the computers she had distributed. She could have sent me the stickers through campus mail, but she decided instead to deliver them in person and arranged to come over to my office. I was excited to see her again. I proudly showed her the progress I had made programming the Apple II. Before she left my office, we had agreed to get together sometime soon.

A few days later, we met for lunch in the cafeteria of the health sciences building. Our conversation was wide ranging, and we discovered that we had many things in common. To our amazement, five years earlier, when I had called Wes Borden about joining his zazen sitting group, Cynthia had been there at his home, having just completed an evening of meditation. Cynthia was indeed the person whose place I had taken in the zendo.

Cynthia and I married in the spring of 1982 and began a family. After two postdoctoral appointments in educational software development, I joined Microsoft in 1990. Busy with work and family responsibilities, I generally lost touch with my meditation practice except as occasional therapy for stress at work.

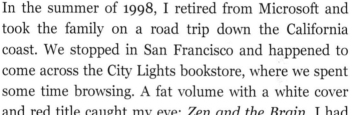

In the summer of 1998, I retired from Microsoft and took the family on a road trip down the California coast. We stopped in San Francisco and happened to come across the City Lights bookstore, where we spent some time browsing. A fat volume with a white cover and red title caught my eye: *Zen and the Brain*. I had not been connected to Zen for nearly fifteen years while Cynthia and I had been focused on parenting. Immediately, I thought, "I really should look into what is happening in the Zen world today." I had always been interested in the connections between Zen practice and neuroscience. So I put down the forty dollars and picked up my copy.

Zen and the Brain, an amazing book by a neurophysiologist, James Austin, who was both a medical researcher and Zen practitioner, became my reentry point into the world of Zen. Reaching the end of the book, I learned that James Austin was living in Moscow, Idaho. I thought, "Well, that's not too far away; maybe I should just call him up and ask if he would mind if I dropped by and said hello." I called and he seemed happy to hear from me. He suggested that I come out to his place and stay for lunch. He lived up in the mountains in rural Idaho, had no computer, and didn't use the Internet. He wrote me a handwritten letter with directions, and I thought, "Wow! I got a handwritten letter in the mail!" He was very gracious.

He was living alone; his wife had recently passed away after living for years with Alzheimer's. James commented that one of the most important things to him in dealing with these circumstances was his Zen practice, and I took note of that. I told him how his book was key to my returning to Zen practice after a long hiatus.

Back home, I did some Internet searches and soon found a website about a monastery on Whidbey Island called Tahoma One Drop Zen Monastery. To my amazement, the monastery had been established by a disciple of Mumon Yamada, the Zen Master I had had tea with in Kobe, Japan, in 1973. Obviously, I needed to visit this place on Whidbey Island.

I still remember the ferry ride and the drive along State Route 525, turning left onto Useless Bay Road—what a great name! I had a feeling that this was an important event in my life, perhaps even a turning point. I had tea in the kitchen with the head monk, Yusan, who gave me a tour of the grounds, including a look into the newly constructed zendo. He told me about the schedule for work parties and meditation retreats.

I started coming over from Seattle to join the monthly work parties and participate in mini-sesshins, the short meditation retreats that began Friday evenings and ran through Sunday mornings. I learned the formalities of chanting and bowing. I learned the ceremony of eating meals using chopsticks and nested bowls. At the end of the meal, each of us used a piece of pickled radish and a splash of tea to wash out our bowls, drinking up the wash water so as not to waste anything, and saving someone else the job of washing the bowls.

One day at the monastery, at the end of a workday, I went out to a coffee shop with Yusan, Shosan (another monk), and a few other people. I was trying to understand the plans Shodo Harada Roshi had for the monastery: would he be coming to live here on Whidbey Island? Yusan explained that yes, very soon, Roshi would be moving from Okayama, Japan, to Whidbey and that this monastery would be his home base. That was an exciting prospect; I cherished the thought of being this closely involved with what I imagined to be such a key development in the establishment of Zen Buddhism in the West.

⟶●●●⟵

Cynthia had discovered Whidbey Island in the early 1990s, when she joined friends for an annual "women's weekend" outing. She fell in love with the place, hoping to eventually move there. She met Vicky Hanna, a realtor on the island who got to know Cynthia over the next few years. Vicky was a superb realtor; she really listened to her clients and kept them in mind when places came up for sale. I had no prior interest in Whidbey Island, but when I discovered the monastery, I suddenly began to take the idea of moving to Whidbey seriously. We started thinking about a "retirement home" on the island and made a list of features we were looking for: We wanted to be surrounded by trees. We also wanted lots of sunshine and a wide-open sky where I could build an observatory. We wanted a place with a feeling of being out in the country, but also close to a grocery—as we grew older, it would become more important to be closer to the amenities of a city. We wanted something secluded but also with a view. Our set of criteria was self-contradictory and completely useless.

I had mentioned to Vicky that I was interested in something close to the Monastery, so on a day when she was showing me some properties, Vicky pointed out a twenty-acre property which, while not meeting the criteria on our list, was located close to the monastery. She suggested that I swing by the place on my way back to Seattle.

I drove up to the property at 6339 Wahl Road in Freeland and pulled into the driveway. A man came out of the cottage to greet me and called, "Hello, David!" It was John Stackley, a man I had met a couple of weeks earlier when we had both attended a mini-sesshin at the monastery. John was serving as a caretaker for the property which was owned by a man named Jon Rhine. He explained that the main house had been used as a retreat center for the Tahoma One Drop Monastery for a couple of sesshins, before the zendo at the monastery was completed. I thought, "Whoa! Really? This very house had been used for sesshins?" Though I have always been skeptical of the idea of "karmic connections," it felt meaningful that I had happened upon a home for sale that had been used by the monastery for meditation retreats. I was starting to accept that some ideas, such as "karmic connections," can make sense in the realm of human experience without making any sense in the realm of objectivity.

Years after the property became the site of Enso House, I wanted to talk with others connected with the place to fill in some of the history.

———⟡⟡⟡———

One of my first interviews in recording the story of Enso House was with Jon Rhine's son, Jim. Jim was a young man in his early thirties with short brown hair and a cheerful bearing. From time to time, he showed up unexpectedly at Enso House to walk the property and reminisce about the early days, when he lived here with his father. We sat in front of the fireplace while Jim told me stories of his early years. He had strong memories of the place, and he was eager to share them.

Jim was two years old when his newborn baby sister died of SIDS. His parents were devastated. The couple had married seven years earlier, melding children from previous marriages on both sides. When Jim was born, he already had three half-brothers; his family felt like the Brady Bunch. But the death of his sister was traumatic, and his parents had difficulty coping with it. Jon began drinking more. Five years later, he and his wife divorced.

Jon was in the brick-manufacturing business. With his headquarters in Kirkland, Washington, he oversaw a plant in Utah. As his business became more successful, he was able to purchase a twenty-acre parcel of rural property on south Whidbey Island in 1988. The property had been homesteaded in the early 1900s. About twelve acres of forest had been cleared for pasture, and a small cottage had been built. A creek through the property had been dammed with an earthen berm in the 1960s. Now there was a pond that he could stock with fish. In the 1970s, a three-bedroom home was constructed. There were sturdy, white fences around the pasture so that he could keep horses and cattle.

When Jim would come to visit his father, he was thrilled to experience the country life: fetching eggs for breakfast from the chicken coop behind the barn; feeding the horses; taking their Doberman Pinscher, Solomon, out to the pond to chase ducks; paddling around the pond with a home-built paddle boat.

Jon Rhine focused his attention on the romantic vision he held for his country home. He took on a major remodeling and expansion project for the house, designing an extension that nearly doubled the square footage. It was a big open space with a vaulted ceiling that came to be known as the Great Room. It had a grand brick fireplace with large figures of an elk, a bobcat, and an owl carved into the bricks. The artist had fashioned the display in Utah. Each brick was then numbered, fired, and shipped to the home on Whidbey Island, where it was reassembled, each brick carefully returned to its original position to complete the work of art on the sides of the chimney.

Opposite the fireplace was an open space that could serve as a dining room, a meeting space, or, as Jon had envisioned, a pool hall. He installed a massive, carefully leveled, premium pool table. Radiant heat was installed in the floor of the great room—a maze of hot-water-filled tubes, heated by a big oil-fired Veissmann boiler in the basement. It made the whole space inviting, attractive, and comfortable. But at the time, it wasn't used much as a family room.

His marriage had broken up and his family was in disarray. Jon decided to leave the house and move to Hawaii. He continued drinking and the situation didn't get any better there. Things continued to spiral downhill, and his heart started to give him problems. Then one day, according to Jim, his father had a dream in which he saw his own father appearing with Jesus.

When he woke up, he felt like a changed man. Determined to change his life, he quit drinking and joined AA. At this point, he was ready to sell his property on Whidbey Island and stay in Hawaii to live.

Jim thinks his father saw an opportunity for redeeming himself in selling the property. He says,

> "I think, for my Dad, it was a chance to have this land go to a beautiful purpose, and have beautiful energy come in and just transform it back to the feeling of why he bought it in the first place.
>
> "This continues on with what you are doing, with positive energy and beauty. Because if you really think about it, people don't come here to die; they actually come here to continue living. And that is what this is about."

A year and a half after we purchased the property, Jon Rhine died in New York of congestive heart failure and liver disease on January 24, 2003.

VISION OF A ROSHI

The gourd flower blossoms.
The phlegm is stuck in my throat now.
Is this the Buddha?

—Masaoka Shiki[6]

S hodo Harada is one of the few Japanese Zen
masters today who works with western students.
His story and his teaching have inspired lay and
monastic students around the world for over thirty
years. He was the first to articulate the vision for Enso
House and has guided its emergence.

Born into a religious family, Shodo Harada had an
aversion to everything spiritual, until one day, while
riding a bus, he encountered a captivating stranger.
The stranger, Mumon Yamada Roshi appeared to glow
with tranquility, unmoved by the bustle of the crowd.
The clarity of his face made others look murky and
clouded by comparison. Shodo Harada quickly
committed himself to become a student of this man,
eventually training at Shofukuji monastery in Kobe.
Although he entered the monastery with great
confidence and enthusiasm, he soon became frustrated
with his perceived lack of progress on the path toward
enlightenment.[7]

He went to his teacher, Yamada Roshi, and said, "I'm leaving. I can't do it here. It's not working. I am going away to sit by myself." Yamada Roshi looked at him for a long time and said, "That's fine; you can go. But what happens if you don't get enlightened?" And Shodo answered him, "I'll think about that when it doesn't happen."

Then Shodo Harada took all his belongings out of the monastery, preparing to leave and to never come back. He says,

> "I went here and there in the mountains, sitting
> by myself, sitting as hard as I could, not
> knowing what day it was, not even knowing how
> much time I was spending there. I just went and
> sat and sat and sat in various places in the
> mountains."

Then one day, he was sitting near the top of a mountain between Yamaguchi prefecture and Hiroshima prefecture. He hadn't seen anyone for days. One afternoon, he suddenly saw a group of people hiking up the mountain. "Are you a Buddhist monk?" they asked. "Yes," he said.

Someone said, "How fortunate you are to be able to practice all day, all week like this! We have to work in the world, so we only have this one day in which to come up onto the mountain and chant the Buddha's name."

Shodo Harada remembers,

"At these words, I was so deeply struck that my whole life was again changed. I realized the deep meaning of what they were saying.

"At that moment, it was like all of my burdens dropped off, as if someone had hit me on the back, and everything was awakened within. I realized right then the mistake I'd been making and immediately went back to the monastery. That day on the mountain, I realized that there was no self to be bothered! I had been crushing myself and making myself miserable, worrying about the problem of realizing enlightenment, when in fact it was found in the living of every single day!

"Everything would come to me even if I did nothing and ceased worrying about my own little problems. Not to isolate myself up on a mountain, closed off from everyone, turning them all away and worrying about my own small state of mind, but to go and be what every day brought to me—that was my practice and the expression of my enlightenment! Ever since I realized that, my whole life has been completely different. I know there is no problem for myself, because there is no one there to feel that there is a problem.

"When I came back from the mountain, I knew what I had to do with my life was to live it totally with the purpose of bringing this crystal awareness to other people. And that's all I really

wanted to do—that was in fact what I had been
doing from the beginning, but I had stifled it in
a small egoistic way. I'd gone to the mountain
for only my own enlightenment; it had been an
expression of my ego. But because of that, I'd
been able to awaken to that greater purpose,
awaken to that greater Self that had work to do
in this world.

"Afterward, my zazen was very different. Before
when I sat, I would do so with a heavy sense of
myself. Now I didn't have that at all, but felt in
my sitting as though I was being lived through
by another great energy. For the first time, my
eyes wouldn't move during zazen but would be
drawn into the floor where I was looking.
During *kinhin*—walking meditation—my eyes
would be drawn into the place I was looking,
and I wouldn't feel like looking around.

"Those things that had been in the way,
obstructing me, weren't there anymore. What
had happened to me on the mountain had
turned my life around."[8]

Harada Roshi received dharma transmission after
twenty years of practice at Shofukuji. One day Yamada
Roshi asked him to go to Sogenji, a Zen temple in
Okayama, to teach and to care for the elderly abbot,
Kanseisan. Shodo Harada went to Sogenji in 1983,
determined to continue Yamada Roshi's commitment
to training western students in traditional Rinzai Zen.
Soon after taking residence there, he requested the aid
of a student, Priscilla Storandt, whose commitment to

Zen training and fluency in Japanese made her the ideal person to serve as his translator. She became his primary disciple and full-time assistant. Priscilla was given the dharma name, Daichi (Great Wisdom), a name generally abbreviated to Chisan.

Shodo Harada's realization of the work he had to do in the world included a vision of a Rinzai Zen Buddhist training monastery in the United States. He instructed Chisan to search for a place to build a Zen monastery within a two-hour drive of Seattle.

<hr>

Michael Lerner is the founder and president of Commonweal, a health and environmental research institute in California. During a United States-Japan Foundation fellowship, he met Shodo Harada Roshi, and they became friends.

On the question of where to locate a monastery, Roshi consulted Michael, who suggested Whidbey Island, just north of Seattle. Several of Michael's friends had already moved to Whidbey, and he thought that the people on south Whidbey would be open to a Zen Buddhist monastery in their community. Michael says, "I thought Whidbey would be a good place because it is one of those nexus points where artists and people involved in moving the culture forward have settled together."

Roshi wanted a place where the people in the community were friendly and supportive. He had been cultivating the idea of establishing a hospice that would be connected to the monastery. Describing the monastic tradition in Japan and the shape it might take in America, Chisan says,

> "The monastery is protected and supported by the community and given things from the community. In Japan, monks go out on *takuhatsu* (begging), where they offer the dharma by giving people the chance to fulfill their need—that is considered giving dharma to the community. Eventually, perhaps takuhatsu is going to be able to be done in America, but not right away. So what can we offer to the community that enables us and them to come together? What can we connect on?

> "Roshi felt that, with a hospice, the monks could really benefit from being among people who are dying. And the people dying would really benefit from working with people who were working on a spiritual death. Monks would find an opportunity to see people dying, which would give them an edge to get their act together in their practice."

—————◦◦◦————

Beginning in 1989 Shodo Harada began making annual trips to the West coast, giving public talks on Zen Buddhism, leading week-long sesshins and visiting patients in the Cancer Help Program at Commonweal.

A group of people in Seattle and on Whidbey Island, including Fred and Carol Olson who had a long time interest in Japanese culture and Zen Buddhism, shared an intention to bring Shodo Harada to the States. One of these people, Brenda Loew (Wajun), who became a key player, had just completed a year-long Tibetan Buddhist retreat at Cloud Mountain in southern Washington. Brenda saw a poster in Seattle about an upcoming event with Shodo Harada and her eye was caught on a phrase saying, "his teacher's teacher had practiced in Tibet."[9] She decided to seek out Harada Roshi and soon became one of his students.

A letter to supporters from Fred and Carol Olson described the search for "a suitable site to build a monastic retreat center to enable Shodo Harada Roshi, abbot of Sogenji monastery in Okayama, Japan, to fulfill his long-standing plans to come to the United States to reside and teach."[10] Listing the benefits of such a center, the letter went on to say, "Part of the longer-term plan and a fulfillment of the dream of Harada Roshi is eventually to provide hospice services at the Zen Center, as a natural expression of Buddhist compassion extending out to the larger community."

In early 1996, a sixty-acre property on south Whidbey came up for sale for $340,000. The group set out to gather funds to purchase the land and establish a monastery.

Brenda had learned, in talking with the real estate agent, that an Asian individual had intended to make a cash offer for the property later in the day. She immediately went to her bank, transferred all her savings into her checking account, and withdrew $10,000 to put up as earnest money. She says, "It was clear to me the land wanted to be used in this way. It was working through me; it wasn't me."

Others in the group were taken aback. Those of a more practical mind thought, "We don't have the money. How are we going to do this?" But Brenda says, "As Roshi knows, that's how it works. You don't plan for it; you let it unfold." She continues, "Practically, it was a pretty stupid thing to do. But it was a beautiful piece of land, and everybody came together internationally. The money was raised."

They signed a contract and they needed to come up with the funds by June 1st. A scramble ensued to raise the money. A nonprofit corporation, One Drop Zendo Association (ODZA) was established as an entity for purchasing the property. George Moseley (Jisai) was put in charge of the financing problem and at the last minute was able to cobble together donations and loans from a number of people to conclude the purchase. Miraculously on June 1st, the ODZA was able to close the purchase using donations and personal loans, all without taking out a bank loan.

A hand painted plywood sign, "Zen Center" was erected on the site, but everyone knew a better name was needed. Carol Olson suggested "Tahoma," the native American name for Mount Rainier. Roshi approved, especially because he felt a connection with native American traditions and culture. Equally auspicious, the first syllable, "TA" could mean "great amount of" in Japanese and "HO" meant "dharma."

Sangha member, Tom Kelley (Mitsuyu), stayed, serving as caretaker, living in a tent through the first winter of 1996-97. A tepee was set up as a place for doing zazen. A yurt was donated where people could meditate and stay overnight while construction proceeded on a kitchen, a dining hall and a small house for Roshi. A building committee was formed and Kurt Hoelting (Shinkai) took on the task of drafting a site plan and shepherding it through the Island County Planning department. Almost all the work of planning, design and construction was done by volunteers.

When the Tahoma Zen Monastery on Whidbey Island was being formed, Shodo Harada asked a longtime student, Larry Zoglin, known as Kyosan to serve as head monk for a year, starting in October 1998. Kyosan has bright penetrating eyes and a shaved head. He always speaks well of others and often surprises his friends and associates with totally unexpected acts of kindness. After eleven years training at Sogenji, Kyosan came to live on the land and work with a few other people to plan the construction of several new buildings.

As head monk, Kyosan was responsible for the sacred duty of maintaining punctuality. Traditionally in Rinzai Zen, the daily, monthly and quarterly schedules are paramount. The rigid consistency of schedule has ensured the vitality of the monastic tradition over centuries. It creates a framework for practice. The commitment to schedule allows for a remarkably smooth functioning of retreats that include many people working together in silence.

Kyosan's first major responsibility was the February 1999 sesshin. His immediate problem was that no building existed yet on the property to accommodate the number of practitioners who would be coming from around the world to join the Roshi from Japan.

With a budget of only three thousand dollars, Kyosan and other community members began a search for a suitable facility, with growing desperation as the date of the sesshin inexorably drew near. The original plan to bring in modular buildings fell through and Kyosan realized he had no contingency plan. He explains,

> "I was really panicking because we didn't have a retreat place. Roshi was coming. We were scurrying around like crazy looking for a place, but all the standard places were booked."

A sangha member suggested an abandoned Boy and Girl Scout camp in Long Beach, Washington, on the coast, a four-and-a-half-hour drive from the monastery. Kyosan and four others rented a van and drove down to Long Beach to take a look.

Kyosan remembers, on the drive back, thinking, "This has got to be one of the worst days of my life!" The place was moldy and dank; there were holes in the walls; it was a long drive away, and it smelled bad. Getting it in shape would take an enormous amount of work and cost a lot of money. Kyosan was feeling horrible—this was a nightmare.

Back on Whidbey, Kyosan continued to scramble. He called Freeland Community Hall plus a nearby motel, a bible school, the county fairgrounds, and the Naval Air Station in Oak Harbor to look at some military facilities that weren't being fully used. Nothing.

When he had all but given up hope of meeting the deadline, Kyosan's attention shifted to a house for sale next door. He approached the owner, Jon Rhine, with what he knew would sound like a bizarre proposition.

"I said, 'This is going to sound really strange so I am just going to lay it on the line. Do you know that there is this monastery being built next door?'

"No, he was completely unaware of that. I said, 'It is a Zen Buddhist monastery and I am there for a year, and we are trying to find a place for a retreat. We were hoping to have it at the monastery, but it's not ready. We found this other place that is so terrible, and we are prepared to pay three thousand dollars for it.'

"So I said, 'Is there any chance that you would take three thousand dollars to rent your place for this seven-day retreat? About forty people would be here.' And I'm thinking to myself, 'What about the liability? This house is ready to show. It is being shown; it's pristine. So what is the likelihood that this guy is even going to want to do this for three thousand dollars?' He says, 'There is something about the way you present this; let me just talk to my wife.'"

Incredibly, Jon Rhine accepted the proposition. His only caveat was that the pool table that had been perfectly leveled, in the middle of the Great Room, would not be disturbed. Kyosan agreed and set to work readying the place. When others arrived to help, the first thing they wanted was to move the pool table to make room for sitting cushions. Kyosan refused to violate Jon Rhine's request. He remembers,

"I realized that we should just use the space exactly as it is. If there is a pool table, then you just put the cushions around it. If there's a fireplace, then you just move with the space. You don't do anything to wall it off; just go with the whole configuration.

"When I realized that we needed to just work with the space, people were skeptical. But I was just so convinced it was possible, I held firm. Then everyone started coming up with these nice refinements, like putting the altar in the wet bar, putting up an *enso* calligraphy against the fireplace, how to work the space as people arrived for the sesshin.

"We went and picked up the Roshi. When we came back, it was all set up with the cushions all around, and the altar was ready. It seemed like this was how the space was always meant to be. It was like, 'Oh my God, this space was meant for a meditation retreat.'

"Jon Rhine had explained to me that, when he built this place, it was really his love, but he never actually lived here. He was sort of inspired by the fact that we were going to use it for some higher purpose, and he really trusted us. When we came inside, it was like this was the fruition of this place. It just had this feeling.

"There was something about the way the mist rose in the morning from the field and the way the windows opened up—it was just like a retreat center, a sacred sort of space."

After the sesshin, Kyosan, Chisan and others felt a connection to the property. Everything had lined up so perfectly in a moment of need that they started to believe that the use of this property for spiritual training was meant to be. Unable financially to consider buying the property, Chisan encouraged Kyosan to simply ask Jon Rhine to give it to them. Somewhat bewildered by this request, Jon Rhine calmly explained that he depended on the sale of the property for his retirement and was in no position to give it away.

When I encountered the property two years later, the news that it had been used as a venue for sesshins suggested to me that there was something inherently important about the place.

GIFT OF LAND

Thus shall you think of all this fleeting world:
A star at dawn, a bubble in a stream;
A flash of lightning in a summer cloud,
A flickering lamp, a phantom, and a dream.

—*The Buddha*[11]

I n September 1990, I began work at Microsoft, developing science content for their new CD-ROM reference products. I found myself riding the wave of personal computer technology as computers made their way into schools and universities and into the entire economy. I had landed at a company that was booming.

I remember driving home from work, listening to the radio and hearing that Microsoft stock had reached another record high; the stock price had split, and the number of shares had doubled. The value of my stock options was reaching levels I had never dreamed of. Doing some rough calculations in my head, I was stunned. My wife and I had never thought of ourselves as wealthy people, but these circumstances were certainly creating some new opportunities.

By the summer of 1998, after working at Microsoft for eight years, I decided it was time to retire and explore some other avenues of avocation. I was fifty years old. I could do more traveling; I could once again take up my hobby of amateur astronomy. Using skills I had learned at Microsoft, I could take on new website and software development projects.

I had been reading Carl Sagan's book *Pale Blue Dot: A vision of the human future of space* in which he says,

> "It has been said that astronomy is a humbling and character-building experience. There is perhaps no better demonstration of the folly of human conceits than this distant image of our tiny world. To me, it underscores our responsibility to deal more kindly with one another, and to preserve and cherish the pale blue dot, the only home we've ever known."[12]

It occurred to me that Tiny Blue Dot would be a good name for an astronomy website. So I immediately secured the domain name tinyblue.com.

In retirement I could explore more deeply the path of Zen practice. Our children had been a huge gift and a major focus for Cynthia and me during their growing-up years. Now as they gained greater independence, we began to look for new avenues of meaning and fulfillment in our lives.

By the summer of 2000, Cynthia and I were ready to meet with an attorney who could help us to set up a nonprofit foundation. We needed a name for our foundation, but we didn't have any new ideas. I came across a quote from the Dalai Lama in his book *An Open Heart*. "If we looked down at the world from space, we would not see any demarcations of national boundaries. We would simply see one small planet, just one."[13]

We already liked the name Tinyblue for the astronomy website, and reading this from the Dalai Lama's book convinced us that the name would also work for the name of our foundation. So on November 13, 2000, we established the nonprofit, Tinyblue Foundation.

In the meantime, I continued my involvement with the Tahoma Monastery, joining in monthly work parties and mini-sesshins. My application for the February sesshin was accepted and participants were asked if they could provide rides to others from the SeaTac airport up to Whidbey Island. I volunteered and soon discovered that I would be meeting Dennis Tucker and Tom Kirchner. I recognized these names. They were the two guys I had met at Shofukuji in Japan twenty-eight years ago. We had a lot of catching up to do.

My discovery of the property on Wahl Road in 2001 fit in perfectly with the new foundation and our desire for a worthy charitable project. I learned that the property had been up for sale for a couple of years, and Jon Rhine had reduced the asking price several times. Initially it was listed for $725,000. Later the price was dropped to $695,000, then to $649,000. At the time I discovered it, the list price was $595,000.

Walking around the property with the caretaker, John Stackley told me that Mr. Rhine was "getting desperate" to sell; in fact, he had not had a single offer. This was duly noted as I took a tour of the house, the barn, and the cottage, before walking out to the pond. It was a beautiful property, though it certainly didn't look like a single-family home. It had a feeling of openness, a venue for events and gatherings perhaps.

John then mentioned that Roshi had a vision for establishing a hospice on the property. My ears perked up: Just imagine—a hospice care center on South Whidbey powered by the energy of a Zen Buddhist monastery. It made me feel that a very rare opportunity was presenting itself.

The fact that there was a connection between this property and the Zen monastery nearby was very interesting. As I thought about the possibilities, I knew this could not possibly be a retirement home for Cynthia and me. Perhaps it could be something much greater. Perhaps we could play a role in making a gift to the community. Cynthia remembers me being quite animated. I described the connection with the monastery and with Roshi's vision of a hospice. There was a chance to do something special. In my mind, the connection with Zen and the fact that Zen training always included daily work periods meant that maintenance of the property might not be too onerous. This was the first time I was aware of my internal faith. If we could put sufficient trust into this act of giving, then perhaps things would find a way of working themselves out, without our having to worry about them.

Cynthia and I asked ourselves, "Does it make more sense to simply give the property to the monastery?" We thought about this for a couple days, but I had a feeling this was not the right way to go. If it were part of the monastery, then it would be in competition for resources with all the other projects at the monastery. I thought it would be better to make it a separate entity with a close relationship to the monastery. Cynthia and I both felt that it was important for our children to be able to make decisions about how the land would be used after we passed away. As the property would be used for charitable purposes, the purchaser could be our newly established nonprofit, the Tinyblue Foundation.

We decided to make a lowball offer of $400,000 for the property. Jon Rhine would probably not be too happy with this, but we hoped that he would be willing to continue talking.

I had this feeling that if it was "meant to be," then it would happen; if not, that would be okay too. My attitude was, "If it falls through, we've lost nothing; if it's accepted, we get a bargain." Now, I was thinking in terms of *meant to be*, a phrase that I have always had a hard time with—what does that mean? Who meant it? I've never subscribed to the idea of some disembodied being out there who makes the universe do what it does.

Suddenly, I was applying the phrase to my own life. Maybe there was a pearl of wisdom in the phrase—that if we don't get too fixated on a particular outcome, things generally work out better for everyone. It's an attitude that is not only practical and healthy but—dare I say—wise.

Saying that something was meant to be is expressing acceptance. Especially if the event is something tragic, like the premature death of someone we love, saying it was meant to be is a way of saying, "Okay, I'm ready to stop my rage; I intend to let go of my obsessive asking 'Why did this happen?' and just accept that it did happen." It helps us to release from our suffering and return us to well-being.

We also tend to hear this phrase when things seem to fall into place on their own. We haven't tried to make them happen, but we feel grateful that they did happen. A person shows up to offer help at precisely the time when the help is needed, or a solution to a problem seems to come out of thin air. In cases like this, we are struck by how interconnected we all are, and how the world is so much bigger than our small selves. We feel that the burdens on us are less—that we can trust in others and trust the world—that things will develop as they will, and that's okay.

A few days after our lowball offer, we heard back from the selling agent that the owner was not at all pleased with the figure. But he did make us a counter offer of $525,000, and we accepted that right away. For Jon, it was painful to sell the property for such a low price, but he also seemed to take heart that the buyer was a private nonprofit foundation with connections to the monastery.

At the end of May 2001, I sent off an e-mail to Chisan describing the recent establishment of the Tinyblue Foundation and our idea of purchasing the property near the monastery. I asked, "Is there any guidance you or Roshi might be able to give us as we consider going ahead with this?"

Chisan replied,

> "Roshi is very positive about your overall plan and wishes to offer his warmest encouragement. And he is appreciative of your consideration in seeking his input as you proceed with the planning stages.
>
> "Roshi suggested that the monastery be allowed a guiding role in deciding what activities are held at the center. The Roshi is, as always, concerned with the one-thousand-year view and the big picture as we proceed together into this huge wonderful vision with its great generosity and vow."

Roshi's advice to remember the thousand-year view came back to us again and again as we moved forward on the project.

I had been sitting zazen on Tuesday nights with an affiliate meditation group near Seattle. One evening, shortly after we had purchased the land, a lovely young woman came up to me during the break and said, "Thank you! Thank you for buying that place." It was Jessica (Sokei), who had recently returned to the United States from Japan.

I thought, "Thank you? Why is this person saying that? I haven't done anything for her." But gratitude had been this recurring theme. Over and over again, people had been saying "Thank you" and I kept thinking "Why? Why? I don't get it!"

To Jessica it was obvious—recalling her time at Sogenji, she says,

> "Well, this is clearly for all of us. Of course there is a great benefactor! That's just the way it works. It appears!' At that point it had been five years of living at Sogenji, a place where everything you need comes from other people, everyone becomes your benefactor. It is a marvelous way to live, actually, because you have no real control of anything yourself, but you are constantly in this state of amazement that things open up and things happen—there is generosity everywhere you turn. I remember Tinyblue was so exciting because of this same

feeling, like a continual surprise—but not a surprise."

After Jon Rhine put his signature on the purchase and sales agreement, we met him and his wife, along with his real estate listing agent. The deal closed on August 10, 2001. Happily, the agent, an avid pool player volunteered to give the table a good home.

Soon afterward, we sent out an invitation to friends and neighbors. It read, "The birth of the Tinyblue Center, a name inspired by a view of earth from distant space as a tiny blue dot—twenty acres of pastoral landscape, a beautiful pond beneath a lush forest, and a wide-open sky for observing the stars. Please join us as we celebrate the opening of the Center, a place for meditative practice, contemplation, and learning on Whidbey Island." The Tinyblue Center was born, and though Cynthia and I only had a vague inkling of what it would become, we were confident that it was "meant to be."

<hr />

The autumn sesshin, September 5–12, 2001, was the second retreat I attended at Tahoma Monastery. Tuesday, September 11, the sixth day of the seven-day sesshin, was a beautiful, sunny fall day. As usual, we woke at 3:50 a.m. and chanted sutras starting at 4:30. Following meditation, we had our breakfast and a one-hour work period, which ended at 9:00 a.m. The schedule from 9:30 to 11:00 a.m. was another three rounds of zazen. Just before the third round, Yusan, the head monk had an announcement to make.

He said, "Unfortunately, I must make this announcement about events that happened this morning in New York and Washington, DC. The World Trade Center towers were attacked, and there were many casualties."

Roshi and Chisan followed the unfolding events on television, and they shared necessary information with the participants. Yusan suggested that anyone who needed to call family members or make arrangements to leave could do so during the break. Otherwise, the sesshin schedule would continue as usual. No one left the retreat; everyone continued to sit the rest of the sixth day and on through the seventh day. Most of us had no idea of the extent of damage or numbers of casualties in New York, Pennsylvania, and Washington, D.C. We waited until we met our families after the sesshin had ended to find out more details.

After the closing ceremony on the evening of the twelfth, Cynthia came and picked me up. She began telling me the details: both World Trade Center towers had been hit by commercial airliners and collapsed. Another plane had crashed into the Pentagon. A fourth plane had been taken over by terrorists and crashed in a field in Pennsylvania after the passengers tried to take control from the hijackers.

She said that TV stations had been showing the same video clips repeatedly of the planes flying into the World Trade Center buildings, of people jumping from the buildings to their deaths, and of the buildings collapsing into rubble. After having watched it enough to get the picture, she shut off the TV and took some deep breaths. Over the coming days, she heard of others who had continued to watch the same video clips over and over again for hours, feeling gripped by the images and feeling unable to turn away. Many children had been exposed to the same terrifying sights and sounds. Among ordinary people, the fear was palpable. The constant replaying of graphic images of wounded and dying people and the uncertainty as to what the future would bring kept people in a constant state of anxiety for many days.

Then Cynthia made a remark that I will never forget. She said, "I was so grateful that you were sitting in sesshin when this happened." She saw our meditation retreat as an island of sanity in a world gone mad. Her comment struck me; it seemed to express beautifully the purpose of our meditation practice.

Roshi's dedication ceremony for the new Tinyblue Center had been scheduled for the thirteenth, immediately following the conclusion of the sesshin. Sitting cushions and chairs were set out in the Great Room of the newly purchased home, and we constructed a makeshift altar with an *enso* calligraphy and flowers. I put a small bronze statue of the Buddha, which I had brought back from Nepal, on the altar. This figure shows the Buddha's hands in a meditation posture, or *dhyana* mudra, the gesture of perfect balance. I found this statue in Kathmandu and have treasured it ever since.

For the dedication, Roshi chose the name Kannon Dojo. Kannon, also known as Kanzeon, is the Bodhisattva of Compassion. *Dojo* refers to a place of practice. A place dedicated to the practice of compassion became all the more urgent following the September 11th attacks. Roshi further explained the meaning of this name, saying,

> "Kannon, the Bodhisattva of Mercy and Compassion, was especially revered in China and Japan. When we ask how the deep awakening of the Buddha is manifested in society, we see it manifested by Kanzeon Bodhisattva.

> "Kanzeon is a name that means to 'see' the 'sounds of the world:' to see the sounds of the world, the pain, the joy: to see those voices. We directly perceive it with our entire being. We feel the sounds of the world deeply, the sounds of pain and joy, and not only of humans but of all living beings, of animals and all the creatures that exist.

> "A Bodhisattva is one who makes a vow to liberate all beings and is also one who lives that vow. Kannon's compassion is a combination of

giving comfort and relief while also taking away pain and suffering.

"It is usually thought that we should be able to have a fifty-fifty balance—that the ideal is to be equal with each person. But Kannon Bodhisattva's function is different. While saying in our hearts we know that balance is best, in fact we each want to have seventy while the other has thirty. No—eighty while the other has twenty, or probably ninety while another has ten. In fact, we really want to have one hundred and the other zero. That is what makes confusion, pain, and conflict.

"Kannon Bodhisattva gives everything, one hundred percent completely and makes it all the other person's. She is like a mother giving to her child. A mother gives all of it to her child, even her own sleeping time. A mother treats her child's sickness like her own sickness and gives everything to the sick child. And when that period of sickness is over and the child smiles again, that is the mother's greatest pleasure. Giving everything and feeling another's joy as one's own joy. This is the wisdom of Kannon Bodhisattva. This is not the world of balancing, but the world of giving everything, completely. This is its function in society.

"In this same way, we take care of people, making ourselves zero and the other person, one hundred. Kannon Bodhisattva knows that we are all originally zero and that original mind is manifested in this encounter. That brings forth our wisdom, and that wisdom takes care of our insecurity, and we cultivate wisdom within ourselves.

"For people to take care of others, and be taken care of at the end of their lives—to do this while cultivating their wisdom—this is the truth of the Kannon Dojo. We have to realize our true wisdom within; that is our responsibility. That everyone's wisdom gives birth to great joy in society is my prayer today."

There was no direct connection between the attack on the World Trade Center and this simple dedication of a place of compassion, but nevertheless, the gravity of the moment was more profound as, in the back of our minds, we pondered what would be the consequences of these acts. Several people at the dedication introduced themselves to us and offered to help make this venture a reality. This is when we first met Charles Terry and Betsy MacGregor, who would serve on the Enso House board of directors.

⬤〇〇〇⬤

Five weeks later, a steering committee of ten people met in the great room of the newly purchased house. We began to discuss some of the obvious fundamental questions, such as, "Whom do we care for?" The evolution of our ideas was a good lesson in letting go.

Ed Lorah (Gentoku) has been president of the Enso House board of directors since its inception. In an email to Ed on September 19, Roshi wrote, "The basic tenet of the Kannon Dojo is that both those doing the caring and receiving the care are people of training... Not just anyone will be accepted."

Several of us expressed concern about what this cryptic message might mean. It was our group's consensus that it would be best to open our doors to anyone who needed our support. The caregiving would be provided by a mix of monks and lay practitioners, but the people needing care might be people with no background in training at all.

After our meeting on October 21, Ed responded to Roshi, asking for clarification. He wrote,

> "It has been my own experience as a hospice practitioner that each person I provide care to might become a teacher to me. Usually the lesson learned is unanticipated, and sometimes it comes from the most unlikely person. I would like us to be open to all possibilities as we proceed, and at this point I do not recommend limiting acceptance to people of practice alone."

Then on October 28, Roshi (via Chisan) replied,

> "Sorry—that was a simple translation looseness. Everybody who enters BECOMES a person of training, i.e., spiritual training emphasis (according to that person's needs and possibilities of course!). The Roshi particularly said that it does not have to be a person who is

already "practicing" but one who wants to use the end of their physical life for that aim in particular... hope this clears that up."

As a committee, we still harbored the idea that we were providing an opportunity for "conscious dying," an idealistic notion that in death we have the option of focused attention, serenity, and bliss. It didn't take us long to realize, once we began caring for patients, that death is rarely so kind.

At this point, many things about the vision and the property had fallen into place. The big looming question was who would be willing to devote themselves full time to pull together all the details and make the hospice a reality. The message we were hearing from Chisan was that Roshi would be moving to Whidbey Island within a couple of years. I conjured up in my mind a vision of Roshi and half a dozen monks, who would be available for caregiving assignments at Enso House, living at the monastery next door. It all seemed plausible.

In these early stages there was a tension between planning and allowing things to happen of their own accord. We discovered that if we trusted each other, what really needed to happen would emerge naturally.

It was a remarkable experience for Cynthia and me to discover how it is sometimes possible to do things by not doing them—to do things by just letting them go in the direction they need to go. This is not about an individual pushing to make something happen. It's about a group of people recognizing a shared vision of what should happen while remaining open to unexpected possibilities. It is greater than any one of us; our own efforts are merely the activity that springs from this shared vision.

It felt like hitching a ride on a moving cart without driving it—just trying to listen and be open as to where it can go. Over and over, we saw people show up just when (or even before!) we realized we needed them. A volunteer physician showed up. A nurse showed up. When we needed remodeling for the rooms to meet the requirements for adult family homes, a local handyman showed up offering to do carpentry. A supporter of the monastery showed up to make sitting cushions. Neighbors showed up to help with all kinds of odd jobs. All these people seemed to appear out of nowhere, and they all wanted to help make this happen. I was awestruck by that and I still am today. Somehow people felt that their own lives were enriched by having a connection with the Enso House project.

The interplay of needs arising and then being met almost simultaneously gave me the strongest sense I've ever had of being guided by something larger. I have always been fascinated by people who live their lives as if they were being guided by a higher power beyond themselves. Personally, I have some difficulty with the concept of a God with a will, but my intuition tells me that working in the world in a selfless way is the best way to be. Those who seem to have been able to transcend their own personal needs, wants, and desires, to work for the benefit of others are to me the ones to emulate. So, I've always kept my eyes open for an opportunity to experience this directly.

When Cynthia remembers embarking on the Enso House project, she recalls a strong feeling of not knowing.

> "It was a totally organic process, a group of people who really believed that it should happen but had no idea how it would happen. It seemed simple and overwhelming at the same time, especially when we thought about the bureaucratic red tape. How is this going to work? There were just so many more questions than there could be answers. But to me, personally, the most important thing about the establishment of Enso House was really learning, at a whole new level, what letting go meant—to let go of control and ownership and just let it happen. At that time in my life, it was a gift and a huge life lesson—of just letting things unfold, of just trusting. Whenever we recognized a need, it seemed like somebody would come along with the needed skill or a talent or a vision."

The emerging project seemed daunting, clearly more than enough work for a full time position. We needed someone with medical expertise to devote their work life to Enso House, but we didn't have any money to pay them. Then Chisan introduced us to a friend of hers who worked as a doctor in Tucson. The mysterious workings that followed brought Ann Cutcher, MD, into the story of Enso House.

COMMITMENT

All paths are the same, leading nowhere.
Therefore, pick a path with heart!

—*Carlos Castaneda*[14]

T he story of the physician who gave up her practice to volunteer as medical director at Enso House begins in the climate of social change of the 1960s, when Wesleyan University decided to try an experiment with coeducation by admitting a small number of female students. Nineteen young women, from neighboring women's colleges, were invited to enroll at Wesleyan.

Among this group of nineteen young fresh female faces was that of Ann Cutcher—seventeen years old, attractive, with wide eyes and jet-black hair. She had always had a propensity for seeking unconventional opportunities—adventure, with the excitement of risk-taking. She was willing to take on the unknown and let it unfold unpredictably.

By the end of her sophomore year, she had fallen in love with a music student. She quit school, married him, and accompanied him to Los Angeles. But their marriage didn't survive the first year.

Feeling stunned and shaken, Ann began to take a long hard look at her options. She thought about following in her father's footsteps by going into medicine. She also entertained thoughts of becoming a potter as she had some experience in ceramics.

Ann had been peripherally involved in the tumultuous college scene of 1968—no one could escape it entirely— and her interest in academic pursuits was at a low point. Having dropped out of Wesleyan to get married, her chances of getting into med school any time soon were practically nil. So the path toward becoming a potter looked more attractive.

While visiting a friend and perusing the library of her friend's father, she came across a book by the Englishman Bernard Leach, *A Potter's Book*[15], which described his experience as a potter's apprentice in Japan. The book captivated her imagination. Ann had never had any interest in the Orient, but suddenly Japanese culture felt magnetic.

Living at home with her parents, she got a job as a waitress, saved her money, and focused single-mindedly on getting to Kyoto, the ancient center of culture in Japan. She was determined to become a potter's apprentice.

A friend of her parents who worked in the shipping industry in Japan recommended that Ann go to Kobe instead. In Kyoto it was too cold in the winter, and the people there were not as open to foreigners. Kobe was an international port city that would be easier to adjust to.

So Ann headed off to Kobe. She left with no contacts or leads for finding a potter to work with—and no Japanese language skills. All she had was a twenty-two-year-old's adventuresome spirit and a wild notion that somehow things would work out.

Within a week of arriving in Kobe, she came across an article in an English newspaper: "*My year as an apprentice in a Japanese pottery shop.*" It had been written by Priscilla Storandt. Ann knew she needed to locate the author immediately, and after a bit of sleuthing, managed to find her.

———————◦⊘◉⊘◦———————

Priscilla Storandt (later "Chisan") had developed an interest in meditation at a young age. One day, she was sitting very still in her room at home when her mother came in and said, "Priscilla! Stop that at once! You're weirding me out!"

Despite her mother's misgivings, Priscilla continued to explore the practice of meditation into her adult years. At the age of nineteen, she read a book about Zen and was intrigued by the connection between Zen and pottery in Japan. The connection felt like a mystery: How was meditation practice related to the stunningly beautiful Japanese tea bowls she had seen?

While in her mid-twenties, a plan began to take shape. She would go to Japan and learn all about oriental art and pottery—how to make vases, tea bowls, and tea ceremony water jars. Maybe she could also find a Zen master who would explain the connection between Zen and pottery.

When she arrived in Japan, she followed a friend's advice to go to Takayama and she located a potter there. When she inquired about an internship, the potter asked Priscilla to demonstrate her skills. Unimpressed by the bowl she made, the man deferred to his father who studied Priscilla's hands and grunted affirmatively. She was taken as a student.

When she began practicing Zen at a local temple, a priest gave Priscilla some fatherly advice.

> "He said to me, 'You can't do two things at once. You either have to do pottery or zazen. Make your choice.' But I was pretty sure I had to do two things at once. Doing zazen was more and more important to me. I really felt a deep conflict. I felt that in order to do pottery, I would have to do zazen. They were not separate. Pottery to me was my original meditation in action."

Priscilla sought out a different teacher and found Mumon Yamada. He was the head of the Myoshinji temple, the center of Rinzai Zen Buddhism in Japan, and President of Hanazono University; he was also the same man I met on my trip to Japan in 1973. When Priscilla asked him her question about Zen and pottery, he thought for a moment and then said, "Pottery—Zen: one path."

Priscilla felt deeply validated by this answer and eventually went to Shofukuji to study Zen while maintaining a new pottery apprenticeship in Kobe.

———◈◈◈———

Priscilla and Ann had a lot in common, and they quickly became friends. Just a couple of years older than Ann, Priscilla lived in a boarding house that happened to have another room available. It was located at the bottom of the hill leading up to the temple Shofukuji.

Priscilla hadn't had any formal training in Japanese, but she did have a natural gift for communication—she could understand the intent of a speaker, and she was able to make herself understood. So without spending time learning how to read and write, she quickly became fluent in spoken Japanese. She arranged for Ann to rent the available room and became her mentor.

Before dawn each morning, Priscilla trudged up the hill to join in the early-morning chanting and meditation periods at the temple. Ann remembers feeling like a puppy dog following her up to the meditation hall before sunrise. Chisan remembers her time with Ann in Kobe as well.

"Neither of us had much money. She would spend her little money each day going to the public bath and eating raw instant Ramen noodles. I would spend my little bit of money walking to the best German pastry shop and buying their cheapest pastry, which is their little rum stick. She was the ascetic, and I just happened to be the one in the Zen temple. But I was the one who was pigging out on German bakery food. She was the one eating raw Ramen. She was the true Zen person. She didn't need to train with Yamada Roshi, but I did."

One day, Priscilla introduced Ann to a renowned potter and Ann was able to secure an apprenticeship. Her first assignment was to pick out little stones from the potter's clay, and she spent long hours doing this methodical, tedious task. It was a useful meditative practice at first. It helped to develop her discipline and focus, and it seemed to be compatible with her personality. But after five years of helping with tedious chores like this, Ann started to feel that she needed to move on.

She felt she needed to contribute something more to the world and felt confident that she could accomplish whatever she set her mind to. She couldn't see herself living in Japan for the long term. At the age of twenty-eight, Ann returned to the United States and set herself to the task of getting into medical school.

First, Ann needed to complete her undergraduate degree which would fulfill the premed requirements. Though she had left Wesleyan University nine years earlier without graduating, the school agreed that if she did a presentation about her experience living and working in Japan, and completed some summer courses at the University of Arizona, she could still be awarded a BA from Wesleyan.

One thing gave Ann pause about medical school—she was not sure she would be able to stomach blood and guts. So she signed up for an Emergency Medical Technician course at a local community college. She was surprised to discover that she actually enjoyed this aspect of the job—the sight of blood didn't faze her.

Ann entered medical school at the University of Arizona in Tucson. There she met and married a man who supported her through her seven years of training. After she completed her residency in Internal Medicine, they built a home together in Patagonia, Arizona, and Ann established her professional life as a physician.

Ann became totally absorbed in her medical practice. Medicine seemed so huge; it took every bit of energy to survive in her practice. Then, her husband had a massive heart attack. During recovery, he had a second heart attack. They hired a live-in caregiver to look after him while Ann concentrated on her practice. This had unforeseen consequences. Before long, the complications and stresses in their relationships became intolerable, and Ann's second marriage came to an abrupt end. Once again, her world had been turned upside down.

———⟫◈◈◈⟪———

About the same time that her husband had his first heart attack, Ann's mother faced a recurrence of breast cancer. In a few short months, it was clear that her mom was going to die. She had been comatose for over a week. Ann had a strong urge to call her pottery friend, Priscilla (now Chisan), to let her know what was going on.

Over the years, Ann kept in contact with her friend. On her frequent trips between Japan and Seattle, Chisan would often arrange to swing through Arizona to visit Ann. She had met some of Ann's family, including her mother.

One day, sitting in the zendo at Sogenji, Chisan felt that she could hear Ann's mother speak. She heard her say, "I'm confident that three of our four children have a good spiritual foundation, but I'm worried about Ann. I want to ask you to take responsibility for Ann's spiritual support." Chisan called Ann and told her the story. Her call arrived just as Ann was going to the phone to call Chisan to tell her about her mother's condition. Ann says her mother died just a few minutes after the phone call.

For Ann it was time to do something she had always wanted to do but had never found the opportunity—to go to a remote part of the world to practice medicine. She went to the Catholic Medical Mission Board in New York City and explained that she was a doctor and wanted to volunteer somewhere. A woman at the desk handed her a stack of folders about a foot high and said, "See what you think about any of these."

Ann started thumbing through the folders, and one folder caught her attention: "Sisters of St. Ann." What could be more fortuitous? Without any other criteria in mind, Ann decided to pick her namesake. "I'll go there," she said.

Before long, she arrived in the bustling port city of Tuticorin in Tamil Nadu, the southernmost part of India, south of Chennai. "I was terrified. I was scared. The chaos was overwhelming. I was sure there was a catastrophe just waiting to happen." To get to work, she had to walk over a river of excrement—she feared that when it rained, she might slip right into it. Typhoid and cholera were rampant, and there were practically no medical supplies. Ann found herself suturing wounds while using no anesthesia at all.

In retrospect, Ann says, "It was great for me. I had no idea what an afraid person I was. I really didn't know that fear was such a big thing in my life." She remembers feeling desperate to leave, spending over a month fruitlessly trying to figure out a way to get out of Tuticorin. The telephones didn't work. There were no computers or Internet, and there were no travel agents, so she couldn't change her return ticket. Eventually, when she realized how futile it was to try to escape, her attitude changed, and she began settling in to just do what the situation required her to do.

Before leaving India, Ann decided to travel to Calcutta and see the work of Mother Theresa and the Sisters of Charity. There she worked in a hospice, but she felt that her high-tech western medical training had little relevance. It seemed that anyone with a high school education and the right commitment would be able to serve just as well. Her most important lesson was that committed people can manage with nothing but the barest of supplies.

The hospice was a gigantic room filled with cots butting up one against the other—a person could hardly walk between them. Some people were bringing food to the patients; others were assisting them to walk to where the food was served. Other volunteers were gathering loads of dirty laundry, stomping on them in the clothes washing area, or hauling the rinsed clothes up to the roof to dry.

Ann remembers sitting next to a blind woman, having no idea what she could do for this woman, thinking to herself, "This is ridiculous—I cannot speak Hindi or Bengali, so I cannot talk to her. Why am I here?" But then it suddenly occurred to her: she could sing. So she simply sang a song her mother had taught her when she was a little girl. "Chicory chi...what shall we be?" And the blind woman immediately connected—a bright smile beamed across her face, and she joined Ann in singing.

After returning from India, Ann went back to work at the Pima County hospital in Tucson. She found a group that specialized in connecting physicians with assisted living facilities, adult family homes, boarding homes, nursing homes, and hospices. Joining them, she visited several adult family homes in Arizona and served as medical director in a couple of hospices. Then, in September 2001, she got a phone call from her friend Chisan, who described a new project connected with the monastery on Whidbey Island that would provide hospice care to people in the community.

⟶◉◉◉⟵

Establishing an end-of-life care facility was not something that anyone involved in the project had experience with. So I began researching how we might actually make something like this happen. Gradually a strategy emerged—we would first establish an Adult Family Home in Washington State. We would need to do some remodeling in the main house—making the bathrooms wheelchair accessible, building a wheelchair ramp up to the front door, and enlarging the bedroom windows to provide access by firefighters. During the next few weeks, I focused on planning the facility, pulling together information about Adult Family Homes and elder care.

I had spent enough time with the project to realize how big it was and how time consuming it would be for many months, if not years. We needed a full-time director. Was I really willing to devote myself entirely to this project full-time for that long?

On October 5, 2001, we received a note from Chisan introducing us to her friend Ann Cutcher. We learned that Ann was a doctor from Tucson who had known Chisan for thirty years. Chisan told us about the two of them going to Japan to study pottery. According to Chisan,

> "When we heard some time ago that we might eventually do a spiritual hospice place, she started to plan around how she could be involved—never guessing that we would be blessed with a place this soon! She is currently working with elderly people in residential homes, as a visiting physician, was working with Mother Theresa's groups in India earlier this year, and has been changing her emphasis from mainly internal medicine to focus on geriatric medicine, in preparation to work on the hospice program when it came to be. Although it was a big surprise that it would start so soon, she has said that she is willing to be the main coordinator on our newly born project."

Recalling when Chisan tapped her for the project, Ann says,

> "I felt, oh, this is just another harebrained idea. The whole thing about hospice was way off the map in my mind. But you know, I think I was just broken apart enough. All my molecules were separated enough. It wasn't that much of a leap to just crack the whole thing open. At any other point in my life, it would not have happened."

When reminded that initially she wouldn't commit beyond six months, she remarked,

> "Of course not! I mean, the whole thing was nuts. I had my life, I had a job, I had an identity. And I wasn't going to jump off a cliff. I needed my health insurance. But I thought, okay, I'll give it a shot.
>
> "And the thing that was so great was that nobody realized that I didn't know what I was doing. None of those people at the table knew what they were doing and nobody knew that I didn't know what I was doing. It was that collective innocence and energy that was so remarkable."

Having a trained physician with experience in geriatrics and hospice work to take on the project would be a huge benefit. Over time I realized that turning over leadership for the project to someone else was best for all of us.

Cynthia remembers the process by which Ann Cutcher took on this new role.

> "I remember hearing about this person who was going to come help us get it going. I thought, 'Well, who is this person? I've never heard of her'. But the instant we met her, I changed my mind. It was, 'Well, okay, of course! I hope she stays.' I remember that she told us she would give us six months. Then after six months, she said she would stay another six months, and after that no one asked her again."

Another individual who was key to the launch of Enso House was Taigan (Tim Tattu), who was living at the monastery. He is a tall six-foot-two man with a shaved head and an easy smile. While working in Los Angeles in the late 1990s doing production design for music videos, he started questioning his life's direction. He says, "I felt that the things I had valued and had seemed important in my life didn't seem important anymore." He discovered Zen meditation practice and joined the One Drop Zendo sitting group in Los Angeles. After meeting Harada Roshi and Chisan, he decided to go to Sogenji for a brief visit. He remembers, "When I crossed the threshold to go into Sogenji, I felt like I had lived there before. And I knew I was going to go back there to live."

After returning to the United States and getting a job to pay off some debts, he returned to Japan and continued his practice at Sogenji for a year. Harada

Roshi gave him the dharma name Taigan, meaning "great rock cliff." In 2001, Chisan suggested that he go help set up Enso House on Whidbey Island.

Ann and Taigan both arrived on Whidbey Island on the same day, April 1, 2002. A group of us met in the Great Room of the main house to start brainstorming about this new project of caring for dying people. None of us were experts. None of us could speak with authority about how to proceed. We had a visit by Michael Lerner, who tried to give us encouragement and guidance, based on his experience starting up nonprofit service organizations.

But as amateurs, we felt as much at sea when he left as we had before. Ann seemed to like the fact that there were no authority figures among us. It suited her personality: she felt much more comfortable having things be a mystery. While possessing great expertise, she is always reluctant to play the role of an expert.

Roshi once praised Ann's work by calling her a great amateur. When I first heard that, I was taken aback, but then I soon realized, yes, indeed, this was one of Ann's most important (and endearing) qualities: she was the consummate listener, always honoring other people's points of view, never using her MD as a trump card to win an argument.

Our committee meetings were productive and never stressful, probably due to the tone that was set at the outset. From the very first meeting of the planning committee, we have always set aside five minutes at the beginning for silent meditation. The planning committee evolved into a board of directors, which continues to meet several times a year. It is a very congenial board to be on. While the tradition of starting each meeting in silence may seem like a minor thing, it has become an important tradition. It sets the tone for the meeting, because it gives us time to drop whatever we may have had on our minds before we walked in the door and to be entirely present during the meeting. The meeting never feels like an onerous obligation; generally it makes each of the participants happy to be working together.

VOLUNTEERS AND BENEFACTORS

Welcome everything. Push away nothing.

—Frank Ostaseski[16]

Volunteers are the lifeblood of Enso House. In fact, the entire organization is run by volunteers: the board of directors, our physician, and our nurse; people in the community who volunteer their time to prepare meals, do landscaping and gardening, help with fundraising events and mailings; and those kind souls who take out the trash and carry loads of plastic and glass bottles and cans to the recycling station. When we needed to remodel the cottage, a volunteer team got organized and worked with a contractor to completely gut the old structure and replace the foundation, the roof, and everything in between. What motivates these people? Why do they feel such a strong connection with Enso House?

When Enso House was being set up, it was clear that besides a director, we needed lots of additional help. As it turned out, nearly everyone who came to work for Enso House did so as a volunteer. Having a physician as our director who was working on a voluntary basis set the tone and modeled the relationship to Enso House for other people to follow. While there are diverse and unique stories regarding how each person has become connected to Enso House, in some way or another, most people either have experienced the death of someone dear to them or have committed to some form of spiritual training, or both. The majority of volunteers are women, but men also serve. I decided to interview some of the volunteers at Enso House to understand the value of the place in their own words.

My wife, Cynthia, serves as Volunteer Coordinator and holds a volunteer meeting once a month at Enso House. She says,

> "One thing that holds the volunteers together is that Enso House is a home. When they walk into it, they feel they are walking into a home where you will be cared for and nurtured. It's the same thing that the families feel who end up with their loved ones here—it's just so welcoming, so supportive, so nurturing, and that's what families need when they are at that point in life."

Another woman, whose friend was admitted to Enso House, experienced the same openness.

> "You feel that for the time your loved one is here this place totally belongs to you. This place is for you. And when you step back and look at the total mission, you realize that it was not only for the dying person and for those who love them, but it is also for the community that holds this place. And everyone is blessed by that."

MyoO

The long-time resident nurse at Enso House, Renate (MyoO), has bright eyes and a calm demeanor. She has a lot of energy and seems happiest when she is doing things for others. When there are no people around who need attention, she finds jobs to do: cleaning up, organizing things, or washing dishes. She loves to be outdoors working in the garden.

Apart from living for a time in Africa, Renate grew up mostly in Germany. She trained as a nurse and worked in a hospital for about seven years. The focus there was entirely on curative treatment, even when patients were near death. Feeling a bit frustrated with a system that didn't seem to accommodate the needs of dying people, she was looking for a change. She had developed an interest in Zen and decided to go to Sogenji, where she studied for a year, beginning in 2002. Shodo Harada gave her the dharma name MyoO in 2007.

I asked MyoO if she felt that her work at Enso House was an important part of her Zen training:

> "I think so; I wouldn't be here if I didn't think so. I don't think I could live in Sogenji very long; it's too structured for me. I would feel like I was in a prison. Of course there are challenges here too. You need to structure your day. You

need to find your own way. You discover who you are in some ways. It is very interesting.

"I'm happy, so I stay where I am. I wouldn't even say this is Zen training. It's just training in life. If you see someone is dying, it's like seeing someone giving birth. You don't see it very often, so it's a very special thing, to see the actual dying. It can show you something. You sit beside the bed and you are just listening to the breathing. It's something very quiet, maybe like a baby when it sleeps. Breathing in, breathing out. There is nothing to gain, nothing to lose anymore. Breathe in, breathe out. You just do it. There is nothing on the agenda that they want to reach or they want to become. They just are there. There is nothing to gain anymore. It is all gone. So the next step is coming; whatever the next step is—I don't know."

MyoO's selfless way of being has set a standard for caregiving at Enso House. In her quiet, unassuming way she has been a model for all the volunteers who arrive at this place.

Ed

Also instrumental in the formation of Enso House was Ed Lorah (Gentoku). He worked as a hospice social worker and in palliative care consultation. Ed spoke to me of his memory of a close friend's death that has stuck with him through his life.

"When I was in my late thirties, my wife and I were friends with another couple who were the same age as us. The woman died—very unexpectedly. She'd had some surgery done; she'd had some kind of blood clotting problem, and they'd put a screen in to catch clots. Then the screen failed, and she died very suddenly. I had had relatives die when I was a young kid. But this was my first contemporary who died.

"We went to her funeral and went to her gravesite, where we actually helped bury her. There was a big mound of dirt with shovels in it. I picked up a shovel and helped fill in the grave. Growing up as I did, all those activities surrounding death were hidden away—they were all done by undertakers in funeral homes. In the process of burying a friend, there is a very strong dose of reality when you drop a shovelful of dirt onto the coffin. There is a *thunk* there. It is the sound of reality. I don't know how else to describe it."

This awareness of how we are removed from the dying process in our culture comes up again and again when speaking to people involved with Enso House.

Betsy

Some volunteers I spoke with recalled witnessing death at a young age and the indelible impression it left on them. Betsy MacGregor is a physician who worked in the field of pediatrics for twenty years. She specialized in pain management and comfort care for terminally ill children and has worked with parents witnessing their child dying. She and her husband, Charles Terry, have been instrumental in the founding of Enso House.

Betsy remembers an incident when she was a college student:

"When I was home for Christmas vacation during my freshman year in college, on New Year's Eve night, this guy Bob, who'd been my boyfriend in high school, was driving drunk, and he drove off the road. My father, who was the head emergency room physician at the hospital that night, was called in. When he was brought into the emergency room, Bob was still alive. My father operated on him all night, but after several hours, he came home, just after dawn, woke me up, and said, 'A terrible thing has happened—your friend Bob is dead. I tried to save his life, but it wasn't possible.'

"I went to the first funeral I had ever been to, and there was an open casket. I still cry now. All the young people from my class were there, and it was so strange to see his familiar face so dressed up the way funeral parlors do— trying to make people look like they're still alive or something, or just asleep. I could not reconcile what I saw with what I knew to be true—that this was the same person who I used to know as a living person.

"I waited until no one was looking, and then I reached over and touched his face, and I was so

82

struck by how it felt—it was just like clay, like this nonliving substance. It was very hard for me to go back to college for the rest of that year, being in psychological turmoil, trying to figure out why this had happened.

"Life goes on as usual, and you don't see any suggestion of this phenomenon—that the people we know are alive, and then all of a sudden, they are gone. All you see around you are live human beings, and you rarely see a dead one. I couldn't compute that this was happening, and to think that this would happen to every single one of these living people, moving all around—including myself. I was really in this existential turmoil for the rest of the year in college—barely hanging on by my fingernails."

Patty

Interviewing Patty brought out the experience of caring for a dying parent. This becomes especially challenging when family members live in different locations and have different thoughts and opinions about caring for their loved one.

Patty is a member of the board of directors of Enso House. She is one of seven siblings who live in Colorado, Washington, and California. Her mother was living in southern California when she was diagnosed with chronic lymphocytic leukemia and lung cancer. Patty and her siblings set up a rotation system of caregiving, each spending a few days or weeks at a time with her. When she began to require more care, they also hired a professional caregiver to be with their mother as needed.

Patty's sister was with her mom when she was suddenly struck by severe abdominal pain. Patty's sister did what most of us would do in such a situation: she called 911 and had her mother taken to the emergency room. No one knew whether it was a terminal condition or not, so she was rushed to the hospital for treatment.

When Patty, in Washington State, was called by her sister, she traveled as quickly as possible to southern California, arriving seven hours later. She immediately went to the hospital. Her mother was extremely frail at that point, still alive but unconscious. It was clear to both of them that their mother was dying. A nurse came in and suggested that they administer a drug "that would really calm her." Patty did not believe this was necessary, because her mother did not seem to be agitated. But they decided to go ahead with the drug anyway. In less than an hour, her mother passed away.

At the hospital, neither Patty nor her sister was clear about what to do next. Patty hoped that there would be some kind of ritual or at least some quiet time at the hospital to reflect on what had just happened. But her sister and the hospital staff were ready to move on. Leaving the body with the nurse, they left the hospital, and the hospital staff sent the body out for cremation.

Looking back on the experience, Patty is filled with sadness that she and her siblings had not been able to discuss with their mother what she wished for the end of her life. She is also saddened by the lack of any ceremony or reflection after her mother's death. Patty feels that their family's lack of experience and discussions limited some of the choices they could have made at the time of their mother's illness and death. Patty says,

> "After that experience, I really did feel called to do something so that this wouldn't have to happen to other people. This is why, when I saw a newspaper article about the efforts being made for creating an end-of-life care home on Whidbey, I contacted the people involved. What a blessing it has been since then."

Sue

Sue Wright is a volunteer who comes in frequently to help with food preparation, cleaning, and whatever else is needed to support Enso House guests or family members. Years ago an experience changed her life—a friend faced a terminal illness and needed help but could not afford health insurance.

Sue's friend, Star, was Director of the Women's Crisis Center in Coeur d'Alene, Idaho. Her only paid job was at the Crisis Center, and her wage was barely enough to live on, let alone to pay for health insurance. So when

Star started having stomach pains, she tried to ignore them, hoping that her body would take care of itself.

One day, Sue and Star had a luncheon date. On the way, Star asked Sue to go with her to the doctor's office to follow up on X-rays that had been taken earlier in the week. Star requested Sue to be present even as she told herself everything was okay.

The doctor came in with an X-ray film and clipped it up against the illuminated viewing panel. He pointed to a dark area that looked like a little football and said, "That's cancer. You need to be admitted to the hospital immediately. We need to do some more tests." Star was admitted that same day. Star's cancer had been growing for some time; it was inoperable, and the overall prognosis was poor.

Sue and four other friends became Star's caregivers and took her home to her small country house, where they took turns caring for her around the clock. Eventually, unable to swallow, she was nourished through a feeding tube. When caregivers could no longer meet Star's needs, an ambulance was dispatched to take Star to the hospital.

"As long as I live, I will never forget the last time I saw Star conscious: she was awake, alert, and sitting up on the gurney as the medics were opening the ambulance door. It had been a very cold night. Everything was covered in a heavy hoarfrost, and the sun was shining in a bright blue sky. There are many trees surrounding our home, and each one was encased in shimmering white ice. The whole world was a shining, glittering, magical fairyland. Star sat totally blissed out, looking around with wonder and awe. To think that was probably the last thing she saw in her life—what a gift.

"Later that night, I rushed to the hospital after receiving a call that Star was dying. As I ran down the hall and neared her room, the nurse was there and told me she had just passed. Star lay sweetly with such an expression of blessed peace on her face.

"Star died at age fifty. Those of us who loved her believe she would be with us today if she had had proper medical care. Her doctor said the tumor that killed her had been growing for several months. Early detection and treatment would have given her a different outcome. Star had no insurance, no job, and little money. She was too proud to ask for help and thought the pain in her gut would eventually go away. Hers is a sad story and unfortunately not a unique one."

Sue's experience with her friend Star gave her confidence that she could serve as a caregiver for people at the end of life. She has been an active volunteer at Enso House ever since it began.

Barbara

Barbara Lamb is a volunteer whose elderly mother passed away in a nursing home. One of the things Barbara found most distressing was the inconsistent use of pain medication. She says,

> "They started messing with her drugs, which they did on a regular basis. They were so afraid that she would become addicted to them—it was crazy.

> "In some states there are certain drugs that are classified as 'addictive' drugs. If somebody has been on them for a certain amount of time— even if they're doing well—the law says, they have to try to cut back. And with my mom, the minute they would cut back—I mean, within an hour of not getting her dosage—she would be whacked-out again. It would take weeks to get her balance back. it was absolutely insane. I would walk into the room and see my mom in pain, and I would say, 'Oh no!' Then I would go talk to the nurses, and they would say, 'We know, but that is the law. '

> "My brother and I then talked to the doctor and said, 'Don't do this anymore. It doesn't matter if she gets addicted. I mean, what are we doing to this woman? She has cancer; she has congestive heart failure; she has psychosis and dementia.' It was painful and awful for her."

Fortunately, working together with the doctor helped to resolve the pain medication issues, and Barbara was able to share some special times with her mom.

> "Some days when I visited, we would laugh and talk, or I would read to her. And other times I would just sing to her because she would be angry and couldn't deal with anything else. But at the end of two years, when she died, my mother knew that she was loved. It was the greatest thing I could ever do in my life—to allow her to know that she was loved.

> "It was my mother's death, and being with her when she died, that made me to want to do hospice work—to just hold that space while it is happening. It was a very sacred space, to be there in that time."

Describing her volunteer experience at Enso House, Barbara says,

> "What I really loved about being a volunteer at Enso House is the incredible appreciation and gratitude for what people do. There is that wonderful sense that anyone who has volunteered in some way will always be part of the place and will always be welcome."

Cynthia Trenshaw

With certification from the National Association of Catholic Chaplains, Cynthia Trenshaw served as a chaplain in several hospitals and at a large nursing home in Grand Rapids, Michigan. Then, moving to San Francisco, she found a new and radical way to practice the Golden Rule. She learned massage therapy and used her skills to serve homeless people on the streets. Among the concrete pillars supporting a freeway interchange, in an atmosphere of diesel smoke and carbon monoxide, surrounded by the din of traffic rushing overhead, people were huddled under grimy sleeping bags on the cold, damp ground littered with discarded fast-food containers, scraps of filthy clothing, empty bottles, and cans. This is where Cynthia came to give back rubs and shoulder massages to disbelieving men and women.

In 2001, Cynthia moved to Whidbey Island. She says,

> "I still had my credentials as a hospital chaplain
> and was looking for ways to use those. I was
> also a massage therapist, but they are a dime a
> dozen on the island. And there is no institution
> on the island large enough to support a pastoral
> care department. So, I was looking around to
> volunteer for hospice, through Whidbey
> General, to do trainings for them or whatever,
> and I heard rumors of this hospice place called
> Enso House. It sounded very unlikely: a couple
> that was giving a house—I mean, who would do
> that? It was somehow connected with Zen. I
> mean, I certainly knew about the Zen hospice in
> San Francisco, but this sounded a little more
> shaky."

Cynthia found her way to Enso House, volunteered her time, and has given countless hours of caregiving to guests. And yet sometimes she feels that she is doing it more for herself than for anyone else.

"One of the dilemmas for me about Enso House is that I would like to be able to say that it is altruistic, that it is absolutely for the benefit of the community, and particularly the guests who come to die there. But, as someone who's been there and been involved in many of the deaths there, Enso House is so much more than that.

"It is a spiritual discipline for many of the people who work there. It is a spiritual classroom for some of the people the Roshi has sent here. I'm not saying that is bad at all—I think it is wonderful, but I cannot say that it is entirely altruistic. I get so much out of it myself. The reason I want to be there is not to help the dying person—it's that I want to be there in those moments in someone's life where the rubber meets the road.

"Death is like birth, and it is always miraculous. I am very selfish about wanting to be in the presence of that miracle as it is unfolding. If I happen to provide comfort or a clean butt for the person who is dying, that's fine—I mean, I'm really glad for that. But the reason I'm there is selfish. So, how do you reconcile that image of altruism, when almost every one of us who has been a part of it feels as if we're taking away from it more than we are giving? Are we taking advantage of the person who is dying? That is kind of the underlying question for me. Am I using their dying for myself? It's really interesting."

<hr>

The South Whidbey community has been generous in donating everything Enso House needs, including food, paper products, houseplants, trees, bedding, linens, furniture, medical equipment, and durable goods, including a large propane-fired electric generator for use during power outages, a new top-of-the-line oil-burning furnace to replace an old one, and a used Volvo. People have come up with ingenious ideas for fundraising projects and have offered their time and energy to make them happen.

We have always been able to find people with the skills, talents, and time to donate to Enso House projects. The original homestead cottage, built on the property over a hundred years ago, was in poor condition. It had no foundation, no insulation in the walls, out-of-date electrical wiring, failing plumbing, and a leaky roof. I had imagined that the best thing would be to bulldoze the structure and start from scratch to build a new house. But a local architect, Ross Chapin, who specializes in small residential designs, saw potential in saving the structure as a residence for the medical director. A local builder, Ken Cunningham, working with volunteers, installed a foundation and put on a new roof. Then we undertook a project to replace everything in between the foundation and the roof, keeping only the exterior stud walls, floor, and ceiling joists. With volunteer workers guided by a skilled builder, electrician, and plumber, we completed the remodeling project in about six months for only thirty-five thousand dollars.

———————◎-◎-◎————————

Enso House plays an important role as a social center, as a community focal point, and as a resource for people who need consultation regarding parents or spouses who are dying. They may just want to come and check it out for when they need hospice care in the future. They may just want to have an outlet for the volunteer spirit that they have. It serves all these roles.

When we were setting up Enso House, we focused on how to create a place to care for dying people. If there were times when we didn't have any guests, would that mean a lack of efficiency in carrying out our mission? What I didn't realize was the important role Enso House could play as a community center and place of information and refuge.

It was an eye-opener to me one summer when I was building the water treatment shed outside. I spent nearly three weeks working on the thing. At the time, there was no guest in residence. But I noticed, throughout the day, people coming in to have a cup of tea and to say hello, and then quietly slipping out. Three or four times a day, people would come over to ask how things were going, to chat or drop something off or ask some questions. I was amazed at how many people were constantly showing up. The success of Enso House cannot be measured by how many guests are there or how long they are there.

Barbara Lamb explains,

> "Something else is happening, and it's kind of a mystery. It's hard to measure. But I have a sense that it is a non-demanding love—a love that goes out and it does not ask anything of anybody."

Relatives of people who have passed away at Enso House and others in the neighborhood frequently come by to visit. They might bring some cherries from their tree or fresh raspberries to share, or they might have some concerns about an aging parent and want to check in with Ann to find out her views about something that is happening.

Ann serves as a community resource person and medical advisor. Even when there is no guest, Enso House is still serving an important function. For Ed Lorah, this illustrates "the roots that we have put down in the community in South Whidbey."

For some people, volunteering at Enso House is as much a personal spiritual practice as an act of service. Another volunteer, Barbara Graham, often works in the kitchen. She explains,

"When there is a guest, we come in here and leave everything else outside the door. That sounds very simple, but of course it isn't. It is a practice I appreciate. When I am coming over to Enso House, it takes fifteen minutes from Langley. As I'm driving I think about divesting myself of what has been going on. I try to come as a clean slate and just allow for things to happen."

Enso House has seen guests' birthday parties, a Valentine's Day concert, a bluegrass concert and a romantic dinner for two. There have been anniversaries to celebrate and memorial services. Once there was even a memorial service for a guest who didn't live long enough to make it to Enso House. The family asked if they could have it there. As my wife describes it, "It feels like a space that allows for whatever needs to happen."

THE PRACTICE OF CAREGIVING

He who attends on the sick attends on me.
—The Buddha[17]

Approaching the front door at Enso House, you see that care has been taken to make a landscaped area by removing a section of asphalt near the house. A thriving Mugo pine stands over some ornamental grasses and lush groundcover sprinkled with red berries. A stand of bamboo grows on the opposite side of the entryway. These plants are all thriving, basking in the warmth of the south-facing brick wall of the house. Someone has built a hand railing out of bamboo, to assist individuals when they take the single step up to the door. Someone's muddy shoes sit on the landing outside. The glass doors allow for a glance at the greenery growing inside the home. No one ever knocks on the door: it feels so inviting to just come in; why would you knock?

When the property was purchased in 2001, the house was equipped with a top-of-the-line security system with sensors on all the windows and doors, an alarm that could be heard a quarter mile away and a system for automatically dialing the police. The hardest thing was for us to figure out how to shut off the alarm and let the police department know that it was just the new owners trying to understand the security system. We soon disconnected the system altogether. Leaving the door unlocked conveyed to arrivals that it really was okay to be there: You are welcome to come in.

Other than a discreet set of pamphlets set out on a narrow table, there are no branding elements of the kind you would see in an institution. It feels like you are entering a home.

There is a little nook in front of windows overlooking the pasture, with a single arm chair. You may not have noticed right away a person sitting there, gazing into the field. Even though they are fully visible, you feel that you should not disturb them. They have found a comfortable place to claim their solitude.

Allan, whose wife's aunt was admitted as a guest, said of Enso House,

> "The minute I walked into the place, I thought, 'I don't want to die; I just want to move in here!' The energy of the place is just amazing. It is an energetic feel. There is a sense of peace and of love and compassion that's being held. It's also cleaner than my house!"

Sharon Parks is a Senior Fellow at the Whidbey Institute and author of several books on leadership and ethics. Sharon visited Enso House when her friend and coworker spent her final days there. The welcoming, home-like space made an impression on her.

"There were times when there were ten to twelve people here, but it never felt like too many. When the grandchildren came, three and five years old, they could skip around here. They were drawing pictures and wanting to show them to their grandmother. It had space for people to be who they needed to be."

Sharon observed,

"The hosts of Enso House were so generous with having available whatever guests needed. People in the community brought food that was welcomed and appreciated. There were soups and breads and salads, and there was always plenty. It wasn't like, 'Oh dear, here is another salad, and we have already three salads. There was never any of that edge of irritation or frustration or ought-ness that you can sometimes pick up on, particularly when people have volunteered in a place and feel that they know 'how it ought to be' and 'how we do things here.' There was none of that. I count that quite remarkable in a place that has to be very wise, very smart, and very careful."

When someone calls Enso House to inquire about admission for a loved one, one of the first things that Ann does is to visit the prospective guest and his or her family at their home. She listens carefully to each person and allows them to express their feelings. Ann makes an assessment of the situation and then lays out all the options: continue to be cared for by family members at home, schedule hospice nurses from

Whidbey General Hospital to come into the home periodically, or move to Enso House.

Enso House is not set up to accommodate patients with dementia. Specifically, there is no way to prevent people from walking away and getting lost or endangering themselves. Also, we do not accept patients who require intravenous feeding or the use of feeding tubes. Every guest must sign a Do Not Resuscitate (DNR) order before they are admitted. This is standard policy among hospices nationally. The reason for the DNR is that a 911 call to emergency services would precipitate life-saving measures that are inconsistent with the purpose of hospice.

During a prescreening interview for Kay, a potential guest, Ann inquired about what things she liked to eat and drink. At this point, Kay was not eating any solid food; all she could swallow now was pureed fruit or vegetables. She mainly drank water. But Ann learned from close family member Allan, that in the past, Kay used to enjoy a glass of white Zinfandel or a Bloody Mary. A few days later, Kay came to stay at Enso House. It was a beautiful spring day, and birds were flitting about in the pasture grass. She settled into her new room overlooking the pasture. There was a bird feeder hanging just outside the window, swinging from side to side as birds jostled for the best feeding perch.

Leaving Kay's room, Ann turned to Allan and asked, "How do you make a Bloody Mary?" She had already picked up a can of tomato juice and a bottle of vodka. Together they scrounged lemon juice, Worcestershire sauce, and Tabasco in the kitchen. Ann had a sip and exclaimed, "Wow! This is really good. I like this!" So as Kay gazed out the window from her new bed, Ann said to her,

"We're going to have lunch soon. Would you care for a Bloody Mary before lunch?"

Suddenly, Kay's face relaxed completely. She smiled and nodded yes. Ann placed a small bottle of white Zinfandel on the bedside table for later.

At Enso House, guests are cared for twenty-four hours a day. That means a core caregiver needs to be in the room or nearby, at least in a semi-awake state. I asked our fulltime volunteer nurse, MyoO, how she does it. "You have done many night shifts; how do you usually do it? Do you stay awake the whole night in a chair? What do you do?" She explained,

> "It really depends on what the person needs. If it's a night shift and I can trust that they will ring the bell, then I can sleep in my room. I turn on the monitor really loud, so I can really hear it. It's not really deep sleep. You can listen somehow with one ear. I have to be very careful that I don't get too tired, because if I get too tired, there is a higher risk that I won't hear it.

"I think you really have to be careful that you get your sleep, so that you make the right decisions in the night; you do what needs to be done and don't make compromises because you're tired.

"If a patient needs more help, then you may need to sleep in the room—like if they have a catheter. We had a patient who was always pulling at the catheter. So we had to sleep in the room and really be careful because she could just pull it out. It really depends on what the patient needs."

<hr />

Families have different wishes for what should happen after their loved one has passed away. At Enso House, Ann and her staff provide the space to accommodate each family's needs. There is no rush. Sometimes it takes hours or days before the family is ready to have the body removed. There are many options: bathing the body, changing the clothes, keeping the body in the room and inviting family members and friends to pay their respects.

When Debbie's mother, Joan, passed away, she decided she wanted to bathe her. She explained, "They brought some very nice lavender-scented water, and we gave her a sponge bath and put on a clean nightgown. We got her all tidied up, and I just sat with her for a while."

Then Debbie thought about whether to bring her young son in to see his grandmother's body. She decided that he should see her because having his grandma just suddenly disappear would probably be more confusing than to see her after she died. She says,

> "I brought him in. Her mouth was open, and I said, 'Well, here's grandma. You can see that she has died. You can tell that she is not really here anymore, even though her body is here. I told him that her spirit is not here anymore.' And he said, 'Well, no, because it came out of her mouth!'
>
> "And I said, 'Yeah, I think that's probably what happened.' So he went in the kitchen, and they gave him some cookies."

After her friend passed away at Enso House, Sharon Parks came in to pay her respects and contemplate her friend's lifeless body. Sharon says,

> "I thought it was enormously important. She and I had worked together at the Whidbey Institute. It was very meaningful for me to see her hands folded and to remember all the things that those hands had done and all the people they had cared for; how many times she had picked up the telephone; how many times she had taken board minutes; how many documents she had prepared; how many nametags she had processed; how many insurance claims she had filed. She had done that with such extraordinary grace. Those same hands had held her

granddaughters. She had been a reader—how many books she had savored! Those hands were now still, and yet had done so so much over the years.

"To have the time to be deeply, personally grateful—honoring, taking that in, and seeing my own hands in new ways. I went to a family reunion a few days later and looked at the hands of my sisters. You know, different features of our experience have power for us at different times. Having her body present here allowed each person to have their own way of knowing what she meant to them."

Kurt Hoelting has a large extended family on Whidbey Island. Thirty years after he rented the cottage on Wahl Road, he found himself back at Enso House, gathering this time with family members to look after his dying father, Al.

"His last night was especially brutal and soul wrenching, but also remarkably cleansing. My brother and two sisters were there along with my mother throughout the night. We took turns holding a vigil by his bed through the night. When he finally died at 6:00 AM we were all standing together around his bed holding hands as he breathed his last breath. It is difficult to describe how much grief and joy were bound up together in those last days. The heart and soul of my father shone through in ways that none of us had seen for many years, if ever—his outrageous humor, his refusal to be anything but grateful, his iron will, and his unflinching readiness to go. We found ourselves falling in love with him and with each other in ways that none of us could have ever anticipated.

"Dad died on February 15, which is the Buddha's birthday. We left his body in the room where he died for the day. After sitting with his body for a couple hours, my brother, Kim and I, and my brother-in-law, Doug went to Kim's woodworking shop to build Dad a coffin. We built a box out of really nice material, using off-cuts of old growth cedar from Kim's band saw mill, pieces pickled with rot pockets that had a natural beauty. So Dad's old rotting body went off into the fire housed in the spirit wood of the Northwest that was also well along on the path of decay. We brought the box back to Enso House, and put his body in it. We blessed him and took turns nailing the lid on the box. We put it into the hearse from the mortuary in Langley and off he went to be cremated."

<hr />

For Ann Cutcher, the intimacy of the dying process often brings people together,

"I think the crucial thing is being allowed into the most intimate of experiences, and it's an incredibly rare thing for strangers to connect this way. The curtains are open, because of the vulnerability. There's an enormous sense of privilege and gift being with a dying person, just as in the delivery room of a baby. It just happens. For me, it's that raw intimacy that is undeniably human and more than human. It is invigorating and sustaining and humbling."

Cynthia Trenshaw helped Ann develop a training program for new Enso House volunteers, titled *Fundamentals of Caregiving*. In the process, she and others realized that caring for a dying patient is fundamentally different from caring for a person who will be going home from the hospital. She explains,

> "There are things that matter, and there are things that don't matter. And there are things that matter a whole lot, things that you don't even think about in the ordinary caregiving class.

> "For instance, silence matters. If you are a caregiver in a nursing home, you can come in and chat; you can make light and talk about the weather, and that works just fine. It doesn't work for someone who is dying at Enso House.

> "People know they are dying, and sometimes people want to process what's happening. You have to allow them the space to do that. It's okay to talk about dying.

> "What else is different? Well, it's okay at Enso House if the guest decides they're not going to eat anything. It's pretty natural. I mean, it's the best way to die. But in the usual caregiving course, you learn how to encourage, how to feed, how to cajole. We don't do that.

"And dealing with infections is different. The immediate aggressive treatment of every infection is not a requirement in all cases at all times, particularly if it is a systemic infection. Just let it go. Of course, the parts of the body are all deteriorating. This is the way the body is going to die. And that is anathema to other ways of caregiving. It's a whole different way of taking care of people when they're in their last week of life."

Cynthia says,

"There is something wonderful about being in a place where death is the expected and the norm, where you can be assured, 'Yes, you are dying. Yep. That is absolutely what is happening to you, and, yes, we will be with you through this whole experience. We won't be afraid of it. You can be afraid, but we will be here and we will not be afraid. We will stay with you. This is what it may look like, this is where it may be uncomfortable, and this is what we can do about that. It's going to be okay.' I think that is a huge gift."

Cynthia continues,

"All I can say is that 'deathing' turns you upside down. As an observer of death, you get turned completely upside down. You just don't have any expectations. That's the spiritual practice. Not to have expectations."

In 2005, Dairin (Larry Larrick) became head monk at the Tahoma monastery. Then in the summer of that year he served as a core caregiver at Enso House for six months. He alternated his work at Enso House with Zen practice at the monastery and found that the two roles supported one another. He says,

"From the perspective of Zen practice, if we're fully, totally in this present moment, with a clear mind, then we can deal with whatever situation comes up. There may be physical pain involved, even emotional turmoil, but because we are one hundred percent involved in it, the suffering aspect and the feeling that there is something being imposed upon us, is completely circumvented—it is just the life force coming through.

"As a Zen student of Roshi's, before I went to Enso House, during my work there and afterward, I was contemplating the questions, "Who is suffering?" and "What is suffering?" and "Who am I?" and "Who is experiencing this whole thing?" That is part of Roshi's curriculum. He likes the idea of his Zen students being at Enso House, to confront them with their mortality, to just be with the situation, whether they want to or not, getting out of self-absorption and just working in this bodhisattva idea of selfless giving."

GUESTS AS TEACHERS

Now that my time is limited, God,
(as it has been all along, I guess)
please look deep inside me again:
see if there is anything left that I need to attend to.
Make sure I'm headed in the right way,
and when my life ebbs from this body, call me
straight into the light of your loving arms.

—*Cynthia Trenshaw*[18]

Jack

In September 2003 it had been two years since the dedication of Kannon Dojo, the home that became known as Enso House. A new 501(c)(3) nonprofit legal entity had been established. All of the necessary remodeling jobs had been completed. We had approval for an Adult Family Home in Washington State. We had a sufficient quantity of medical equipment, including motorized hospital beds, walkers, and wheelchairs. Our core caregivers, all volunteers, a physician, a nurse, and an assistant from the monastery were all on board. Now all we needed was our first patient, or "guest."

Roshi was back on Whidbey Island leading the September sesshin of 2003, and there was a feeling of expectation in the air.

Jack lived at Possession Point, a promontory overlooking the waters of Puget Sound. Heavily forested with Douglas fir, western hemlock, and western red cedar on the southern tip of Whidbey Island, Possession Point affords a magnificent view of Mount Rainier. A road runs down to the beach, a narrow stretch of gravel covered with driftwood. A couple dozen homes are perched between the beach and a steep cliff behind them. They are linked together by a meandering pathway called Possession Beach Walk.

Before moving to Whidbey Island, Jack had lived a rich and varied life. He had been a professional musician in a symphony orchestra, an author, and an explorer, climbing mountains in Alaska and meditating in remote caves. Jack was not one to engage in small talk, and he didn't socialize much in the community. He preferred to work alone and pursue his passion for writing poetry. He seemed to have boundless energy, doing odd jobs and mowing lawns. He hand-built a breakwater out of creosote logs he had salvaged on the beach.

Originally, Jack built himself a shack up among the trees on the edge of a cliff. It was only accessible by a series of ladders and ropes. One winter, heavy Northwest rains loosened the soil under the dwelling, causing the shack to slide down to the beach. Fortunately, he wasn't inside at the time.

Then Jack built a new house from recycled materials at the far end of Possession Beach Walk, tucked up into the cliff, among the blackberry, vine maple, and red alder. He added a loft for his bed. A bookshelf on the wall served a dual purpose: it held his many books and served as a ladder to the loft.

Jack managed just fine without electricity or plumbing or running water. He kept to himself and didn't say much. Then, Jack was diagnosed with lung cancer. A few of his friends came to his aid, but as Jack grew weaker, taking care of him became an increasingly challenging task.

Jo and Jim Shelver are longtime community activists who never hesitate to volunteer for community projects and are often the first to help out their neighbors when the need arises. They offered to help with his caregiving.

Another woman, Gaea, is a registered nurse on Whidbey Island. She likes to work independently, on her own schedule. At the time, she was staying in Jo and Jim's home on Possession Beach Walk.

When Gaea first met Jack, she was put off by him. When she was growing up, several family members had smoked, and two of them eventually died with emphysema. Gaea had a strong aversion to tobacco, and Jack had a smoking habit. Jack certainly wasn't the kind of person that Gaea would have sought out. But Jo and Jim had a way of bringing in volunteers by appealing to their kindheartedness and generosity. So Gaea soon found herself committed to caring for Jack. In fact, before long, she became Jack's primary caregiver.

As the caregiving demands increased, Gaea needed to find others to help out. She was a member of a Circle of Caring group that had been formed to support each other as they got older. At the next meeting, she said, "You know, we sit around talking about caring for people when they get sick, but I need help! There's this guy who needs care, and I cannot do it myself."

Two people from the Circle of Caring group volunteered. But Gaea had a previous commitment to be away for a week. Suddenly, she needed to organize a caregiving team.

She invited volunteers to come down to Jack's place to meet him. Gaea would leave them alone with Jack for half an hour or so. Jack rarely spoke a word; generally, he said nothing the whole time. Some people felt uncomfortable with his silence, but others volunteered.

There was a cabin not far away that had running water and electricity, and the owners weren't there for most of the year. Jim got their permission to connect a hose to a faucet and run a long extension cord from an outlet of their cabin. It was enough to set up a small lamp to run a radio in Jack's house.

Jack was too weak to climb the bookshelf ladder to the loft anymore, so Gaea and Jim rigged up an old canvas army cot he had found in his garage, a wooden door for support, and a Costco trifold mattress on top to make a bed that stood on the floor. There was precious little space between the improvised bed and the opposite wall.

After having put together a schedule for caregivers for Jack, Gaea took off for her trip. When she returned a week later, she found that more help was needed; caregiving had grown too difficult. She knew it was time to consider Enso House and explained to Jack that they had been waiting for their first patient. He would be doing them a service by being their first guest. Plans were made for him to go to Enso House the next day.

Soon, Ann and MyoO and Taigan arrived from Enso House. Taigan wanted to make sure that Jack had his wallet and his ID, but he discovered that Jack had apparently been living contentedly for years with a San Francisco Library card as his only ID.

Jo and Jim used their gas-powered golf cart to transport him. Jack was carried down from his house and loaded into the golf cart. Jo drove the cart while Taigan held Jack, and the others walked behind, winding past the beach homes and the curious eyes of the neighbors, making their way to the parking lot. They helped Jack into the car and drove him to Enso House.

As Gaea spent more time with Jack, she gradually developed a fondness for him.

"He didn't speak much at all. Just his presence—he would look you straight in the eye. It was like receiving *darshan* (blessing). In fact, he was a gentle soul. I learned to appreciate him. Oftentimes when getting to know someone, words get in the way. I felt like being with this person, who was just present and didn't speak much, I was really able to get to know him."

The day that Jack arrived at Enso House, I had a chance to meet him briefly myself. MyoO had pushed his wheelchair outdoors, where Jack could enjoy the vista of the pasture and the pond. Greeting him, I was immediately taken by his gaze. His penetrating eyes made me feel that it was pointless to hide anything from this man: it was impossible to put on any airs or feign any niceties. I simply thanked him for coming to Enso House.

One of the Enso House volunteers at the time was Kitty, an eighty-year-old woman who had shown up at the monastery a couple of years before and participated in sangha activities, including sesshins. She had over twenty years of meditation experience that included years in Sri Lanka and Thailand. Kitty was an excellent cook and prepared many wonderful meals at Tahoma and at Enso House.

Kitty loved to keep birds and had a cockatiel that she was quite fond of. She named him Karuna, which is the Sanskrit name for "compassionate service." Nicknamed "Runi," the bird loved to sit on Kitty's shoulder and go wherever Kitty went. But Kitty was serving as *Tenzo* (cook) for the September 2003 sesshin at Tahoma, and birds were not allowed in the kitchen, so Runi took to riding on MyoO's shoulder at Enso House.

As Jack was lying in bed at Enso House, Runi hopped from MyoO's shoulder onto Jack. The bird would sit on his toe or his shoulder or the top of his head. Jack felt quite comfortable with the bird on his body. As a child, he had kept birds and felt an affinity for them.

If any crumbs dropped into Jack's beard, Runi would be there instantly to fetch a bite to eat. The bird was very insistent about staying with Jack—Runi really didn't want to leave. MyoO and Ann were awestruck and impressed by the bird's behavior. Others were taken aback.

Eventually, it was decided that it would be best for the bird to be put in a cage in the solarium, the big sunny space adjacent to Jack's room. But the bird protested loudly and persistently. It sounded like Runi was going berserk.

Jack had a twelve-year-old female cat that he loved. Jack had worried about what was going to happen to her after he died. Gaea had promised him that she would make sure that his cat had a home, but now that he was out of his house, she really didn't know what she was going to do with the cat. She knew of an animal communicator, a woman by the name of Jacqueline, who lived on Whidbey. Gaea called up Jacqueline and explained the situation. They arranged for Jacqueline to come over to meet the cat to see if she could find out where the cat would like to go after Jack died. But at the scheduled time, she didn't show up—she had gotten lost. So she called and apologized, "Sorry; I couldn't find the place. Can we do it on Monday?"

Before Gaea hung up the phone, she asked Jacqueline about Runi's strange behavior. She explained, "We have this bird that just doesn't want to leave him and complains loudly when we separate them."

Jacqueline asked, "Well, what's the bird's name?"

"Karuna. We call him "'Runi."

According to Gaea, animal communicators don't need to be physically present with the animals in order to communicate with them.

When Runi was separated from Jack, he began squawking and carrying on, obviously upset. But as soon as Jacqueline started communicating with him, he suddenly became absolutely silent. Jacqueline described what she picked up as Runi's thoughts. She said that Runi wanted Jack to focus on a point three feet above him and imagine spreading his arms like wings and taking flight, as if he were leaving his body.

Gaea asked, "Would you be willing to tell Jack this now?" She held the phone to Jack's ear while Jacqueline talked to him. That was the day before Jack died.

Around ten o'clock that evening, as Gaea was about to leave, she said to Jack, "Well, I'm leaving. Remember the message from Runi that you're supposed to focus on that point three feet above you and imagine taking flight."

When she got a call from Ann early the next morning, she went directly over to Enso House. Gaea went into Jack's room and was alone with him. She took his hand and said, "Okay, I'm here now." Then the two of them breathed together. She reminded him to focus on the point and imagine himself taking wing. Then he consciously left his body.

Fortunately, an old friend of Jack's offered to provide a home for his cat.

Cynthia Trenshaw served as one of Jack's caregivers. She remembers how important it was for him to avoid unnecessary talk.

"I stopped by to say good-bye to him. That was a very moving experience, the experience of saying good-bye to him, and to thank him for

what he taught me through his silence. He
insisted on silence, and it was a feet-to-the-fire
kind of thing, his silence. He needed silence,
and you had to be comfortable with the silence,
or he would throw you out. He was quite a
teacher."

The day before Gaea was about to leave for a week,
Jack asked her to bring him his checkbook. Gaea said,
"No, Jack." But Jack insisted and tore a check out of
the checkbook. He could barely write, but he managed
to scribble the check. He didn't show it to Gaea; he just
put the check in an envelope and sealed it.

A week later, Gaea opened the envelope and looked at
the check. It wasn't written as a check at all. He had
simply used it to write a note for Gaea. Most was
illegible, but he said, "I love you, and I'll miss you." To
Gaea, this note was much more precious than money.

Taigan remembers Jack as a very special person.

"Jack was one of the few people I have ever
cared for who was able to think about others
while he was very sick and dying. He really gave
you the feeling that he was holding your hand—
you weren't holding his hand. And you got the
feeling he was comforting you through this
experience. It was very powerful for everyone
who was involved. I think everyone who was
caring for him realized there was something
special about him."

For the first several years, I was content to serve as support person for Enso House, without being involved in direct patient care. Then, as I saw my father's health declining, it occurred to me that I might soon find myself close to end-of-life care. When Ann announced that she would be giving another Fundamentals of Caregiving class, I decided it was time for me to take the course. By becoming certified as a nursing assistant, I could help Ann and MyoO with patient care.

From the course, I was struck by how different the hospice perspective is from the medical treatment point of view. In the hospice perspective, death is accepted: we focus on palliative care to reduce pain and anxiety, but we do not attempt to slow down or halt the dying process. All efforts to cure the patient have been terminated. Through this acceptance of the inevitable, the focus changes in a profound way. All the energy that had been directed toward postponing death is now available to focus on being with loved ones, sharing forgiveness, and saying good-byes.

Death arrives for each one of us in different ways: our energy reserves may be depleted after we stop eating; our lungs may fill with fluid, making it impossible to breathe; our heart muscle may die when its blood supply is cut off; our bodily systems may shut down from a bacterial infection; we may bleed to death from an internal hemorrhage. These are the natural ways we have always died.

Upon being admitted to Enso House, a patient signs a Do Not Resuscitate order. A patient who has difficulty breathing will not be taken to an emergency room and connected to a ventilator. A patient whose heart goes into fibrillation will not receive an electric shock. If an infection occurs, antibiotics may or may not be given depending upon the patient's wishes. Neither intravenous feeding nor feeding tubes will be used.

In a medical setting, of course, all of these treatments would be used to treat the patient. But at the end of our lives, such treatments can cause more suffering than relief. The trauma of being rushed to an emergency room and hooked up to a ventilator and other equipment sometimes makes things worse. When the body is shutting down, the digestive system weakens and often cannot process additional fluids and nutrients from artificial feeding systems. In a hospice setting, cure is no longer the goal—the relief of suffering is. With this perspective, the opportunities for a peaceful transition are much greater.

Joan

Joan came to be a guest at Enso House in 2003. Her daughter, Debbie, had managed Joan's care before she arrived at Enso House. I sat down with Debbie to hear the story of the end of her mother's life.

Joan had various health issues. She was dying of congestive heart failure but also had back pain as a result of a tumor in her vertebrae and a surgery she had undergone to remove it. Debbie contracted with a for-profit hospice on the island to administer homecare for her mother.

Although the people from hospice were committed to working with Debbie to deliver the care Joan needed, there were regular complications with the pain management aspect of her mother's care. When Joan needed additional medication, Debbie had to travel to the pharmacy to get it, but sometimes the pharmacy was out of that particular medication. In an effort to control her pain, Joan was first given the pill form of medication, then the liquid form, and eventually, a patch was used. This helped to relieve some of Joan's agitation.

A decade earlier, Debbie's father was dying, and his wife was acting as his caregiver. In that case, it was very important to Joan that her husband be spared the wooziness of pain medicine. She wanted him to be clearheaded and conscious enough in case he wanted to say anything in his last days. It had been difficult for Debbie to watch her father in pain while her mother chose alertness for her husband over deadening pain.

That experience now complicated Debbie's decision-making for her mother.

"I knew how she had felt about my dad, how she had wanted him to be clearheaded, and I knew that she wanted to be clearheaded too. It's pretty hard when you're watching someone in agony, and staying clearheaded is the most important. It seems funny to even think about it now, but at the time I really knew she didn't want to be too out of it."

As her mom's needs for care grew, Debbie hired three women in their mid-sixties, through Island Home Nursing to care for her mom during the daytime. As her mom became frailer, she needed more help, and the caregivers needed to come every day.

Before long, her mom started to confuse the normal day and night schedule, becoming active at night, wanting to walk around, use the bathroom, and bust herself at all times of the night. Soon it became clear that even three caregivers was not sufficient; someone was needed to assist during the night who would remain alert and look after her. Island Home Nursing was having trouble finding workers.

Debbie wanted to meet each of the caregivers and introduce them to her mom while she was conscious and relatively free of pain. But it became increasingly difficult to manage all the caregivers. While the original three ladies stayed on, doing caregiving during the day, there always seemed to be new people at night, and Debbie found it disturbing because she could not follow the staff rotations closely. Her son was five years old at the time and had to get up early in the morning to go to school, so it became increasingly challenging to juggle the demands of a young child and an elderly mother.

Her mom's pain was worsening. Even with visits by Whidbey General Hospital hospice nurses, they could not get her pain under control. Joan needed higher and higher dosages of oxycontin. Getting the right quantities of a highly regulated narcotic like this requires multiple trips to the doctor and the pharmacy. Trying to juggle all these aspects of urgent care, Debbie was feeling exhausted and unable to spend any quality time with her mother. Then one of the hospice nurses told Debbie about Enso House and Debbie said she would think about it.

> "And just the next day, when I was at my mom's place, my son's school called my work and said, 'You know, Debbie hasn't come to pick up her son.'

> "It was a half-day at school, and I had completely forgotten my son! And I just dissolved into tears, because it was like everything was falling apart."

Debbie called Enso House that day. Immediately after her mom moved there, Debbie felt the heavy burden of responsibility lift and was finally able to relax and be with her mom. She says,

"My son, Joel, was five. He would come and see his grandma for a little while and then go to play Pokémon. We had brought a Pokémon animated DVD. MyoO showed him how to put it in the DVD player.

"I sat with Mom for a while and then went out to see how he was doing. There they were, all out there—Ann, Taigan, MyoO, and Joel—all totally immersed in a Pokémon video. I thought, 'This is great!' Somebody was watching him, and they were having fun too. It was so sweet!"

Debbie told Ann that she hoped to be present when her mother passed away. One evening, Ann called her to let her know that her mother's breathing had changed. Debbie thought, "Oh my God, it's really going to happen!" Debbie recalls,

"I got there, and Ann, Taigan, and MyoO were all gathered around Mom. I talked to Mom and held her hand, and then she died. It was very peaceful. She breathed a little bit, and then she didn't. And I was so glad to be there; I was so glad—after all that time of looking after her—to be able to hold her hand as she took her last breath. What a gift."

Gene

Gene, a seventy-one-year-old man, moved to Whidbey Island to be close to his sister, Sue, thirteen years younger. He was generally fit and strong; he had a habit of walking two to three miles every day. Every week or so, Gene would take the bus into Freeland to buy groceries. On these occasions, Sue would meet him to spend some time together. "We would go out to lunch or coffee, or go traipsing around the island, looking for something new; we would go and just pal around."

Sue is a tall, self-assured woman who listens well and speaks confidently. I was impressed by her strong intuition when helping her brother make decisions at the end of his life. She says, "Everybody who ages needs help at some point, even if it is just getting groceries or doing a little cleaning or finding out how to do something like Medicare Part D."

One day, Gene was aware of something going on in his stomach area. He went in to have it checked. He was told to come back in three weeks to readjust his blood pressure medicine. Sue thought, "That doesn't seem right. What has that got to do with a stomachache?"

Three weeks later, he returned to the doctor who sent him to the hospital for a CT scan. After analyzing the scan, they immediately called Gene back in and told him he had pancreatic cancer. Sue explains,

> "After that diagnosis, it was another two weeks before he was able to see a cancer specialist at Providence Hospital. He had two rounds of chemo. He was bleeding internally and ended up in the hospital for blood transfusions. He

went in for a third round of chemo, but by the time he got there, his skin had turned yellow; his liver was failing. They couldn't give him any more chemo, and it was already too late for surgery.

"So from the time the doctor diagnosed him to the time he died was about nine weeks. His disease progressed very fast. It makes me think: each one of those days he had to wait was a precious day where it got worse. I think you really need to have someone on your side, an advocate, when you are older."

Joanie was Gene's partner for forty years. Joanie was a free spirit, and Gene was attracted to her quality of spontaneity. When Gene became ill, Joanie, who was already ill herself, became paralyzed by anxiety. Fortunately, Sue was there to step in.

"They were living in a small, two-bedroom apartment in Langley, just the two of them. Joanie was trying to take care of him when I wasn't there. I was bringing them groceries, picking up meds, trying to get him to eat something, which he wasn't doing. I was getting Meals on Wheels to come in, and Whidbey Home Health nurses were coming in once a week.

"Then I got a phone call from them early in the morning. Gene said, 'We need help. Joanie cannot get out of bed; there is something wrong with her back. I can't help her, and I can't get out of bed.'

"The Home Health nurse met me at Gene's. She began taking his vitals and then called Ann at Enso House. Her voice was urgent. Ann said, 'You can get him here this afternoon.' The nurse ordered a cabulance to pick him up at three o'clock. So that's when Gene came to Enso House."

Sue was relieved that Gene had found a place consistent with his style. She says,

"Gene would have been absolutely mortified to wake up and find himself in a nursing home, because that's not the way he lived his life. He was a classy person. He wasn't one of those people who would just throw a TV dinner in the microwave and say, 'here's dinner.' No, they had candles and they had placemats. They had flowers or a little plant or something. He lived his life that way.

"He liked the old-fashioned ways of doing things, like dining cars and trains and linen tablecloths and silver. Even his candles: he didn't go to the dime store and buy twenty-nine-cent candles. There were always really nice burning candles that didn't drip all over the place.

"Enso House was the perfect place for him. It would have been a lot harder if he'd been at a nursing home. I would have been frantic actually, to have all of those people coming in and out and poking him and prodding him. The old person down the hall might be screaming their head off. He would have been just mortified by all of that."

When Gene arrived at Enso House, I had recently completed the Fundamentals of Caregiving course, and my wife, Cynthia, had completed the course years earlier. We both offered to help with Gene's care, and Ann put us on the schedule.

A couple of days after meeting him, I said hello to Gene as I came in to volunteer. He greeted me with a strong handshake, and he remembered my name. His hands and feet were both swollen and puffy. The top of his head was bald; the skin had a distinctly yellowish cast to it. The whites of his eyes were jaundiced.

Waves of confusion swept across his face like passing clouds. "Where is my chapstick?" he asked. Ann and I searched under the bed and among the bed clothes. Finally, we found the lip balm in the wastebasket. How did it get there?

Gene declared, "The cart is in the wrong place!" Earlier it had been beside the bed; now it was at the foot. At the foot of the bed, it gives caregivers more ease of access to the patient. But it wasn't where Gene wanted it. We rearranged the bedside table and lamp and moved the cart back to where Gene thought it should be. Later, Ann explained to me that as people lose more and more control over their life, it's not uncommon for them to obsess about controlling various small things.

The confusion passed, and Gene asked me what I did for a living. I told him I was a teacher of physics and worked in software development. I asked him about his work. He told me, years ago, he was the artistic director of a theater company, The Brass Ring, in Seattle. Later, he managed an apartment building in San Francisco. We talked a bit about San Francisco.

He was lying down but indicated that he needed to get up and relieve himself. It was my job to assist him. I leaned over to help him sit up. He was a big man, over six feet tall and around two hundred pounds (Ann reminded me later that we should have raised the bed first, to reduce the risk of me throwing out my back). After he sat up, he paused to catch his breath—that effort alone was exhausting.

After he was done, I cleaned up some diarrhea that had soiled the edge of the bed. A mat beneath him took up the bit of spilled urine. It was a dark brown color: another indication of liver failure. Either the cancer had taken over his liver, or the cancerous tumor on his pancreas had blocked ducts to the liver, making it nonfunctional.

The next day, Gene was considerably weaker. He was restless, tossing and turning, wanting to sit up, then almost immediately needing to lie down again. Ann was up all night with him; he never slept for more than five to ten minutes at a time.

Lying in bed, Gene tried to sit up every few minutes. We helped him slide his legs off the side of the bed. I put my hands around his shoulder and cradled his head as I lifted him up to a sitting position. He could just barely balance and steady himself with his arms, and he tired quickly.

As he lay in bed, fidgeting, I could easily identify with him and imagine myself in his body. My usual nightly ritual is to flip back and forth in bed between my left side and my right, trying to get comfortable before I fall asleep. This often results in bedding and sheets getting tangled up around my feet, which is exactly what was happening to Gene. I could feel his restlessness and the constant itch to move.

Gene was mostly incoherent. We applied water to his chapped lips with a saturated swab and he relished sipping from a syringe. He wasn't able to suck a straw anymore. The skin of his whole body was yellowish. His eyes would move around without focusing on any one thing in particular. From time to time, his eyes focused on my face momentarily. At one point, our eyes met. I grinned, and a quick smile flashed across his face.

Unsure if I should say anything, I asked him, "How are you feeling, Gene?" His eyes locked onto mine, he paused and said simply, "Just look!" It was a good lesson for me; how would I respond, on my death bed, if someone were to ask me how I felt?

Watching Gene, I could remember how it feels to be ill, perhaps nauseated, or feverish. At those times my awareness is in my body, and I feel that the best I can do is just inhale and exhale and endure; my awareness of others is blocked. My single-minded coping strategy is simple: just let me get through the next breath without additional pain; just let me exhale this breath and expel the pain. Don't distract me with useless talk and carrying on. I could identify with Gene. This was serious. This was impending death.

I was reminded of an exchange with Roshi at *sanzen* (individual interview) during one sesshin. In the previous rounds of zazen, I had been feeling extreme pain in my legs that seemed unbearable. When I told Roshi how much I was hurting, he simply reminded me that the guests at Enso House experience even worse pain, and they have no opportunity for relief at all. He was right. My pain on the cushion was temporary. It wasn't causing any damage to my muscles or joints. I needed to make some adjustments to my attitude. In subsequent rounds of sitting, remembering the patients at Enso House, I had slightly more equanimity perhaps. Perhaps not.

The muscular features of Gene's arms and shoulders had transformed into flaccid skin and shriveled bones with loosely hanging flesh. The bit of strength still remaining in his arms could only be summoned with intense determination. His muscles shuddered as he tried to balance himself on the edge of the bed. His lower body seemed swollen—his skin covered a growing mass of tumor tissue just beneath the surface. The amazing thing was that he could still present himself as a conscious human being while his body was riddled with rapidly growing cancerous tumors.

I could feel myself inside of Gene's body. I felt the pressure of the inexorable growth of the disease. I felt his exhaustion; I felt his determination to take a deep breath and face this onslaught; I felt the concentration to summon the words from the English language to express my wants and needs: "Get me up! Water!" I felt the verbal explosions that bypass all thinking, all planning, all cogitation: "Stop! That hurts!"

Gene's sister had been amazed at how quickly Gene's illness progressed. She knew how important it was for Joanie to come visit, so she called the nursing home.

> "I called Careage, the nursing home and said, 'I need to get her to Enso House to say goodbye to Gene, because he is not going to last very long.'"

They prepared Joanie and drove her over, got her into her wheelchair and wheeled her in. Gene responded instantly. They spent the whole day together. So Joanie was able to be with him one last time. She repeatedly called him "my beautiful man."

Gene and Joanie had a good visit, and then at six, Sue took her back to the nursing home.

Finally it became clear that Gene wasn't going to live much longer. He seemed to be comfortable, but he was hardly breathing. Sue says,

> "I think he was aware of things going on around him, that I was coming in and out. I had gone home to do something, and at two o'clock, for some reason, I had this real urgency to come back. At that point, I knew it was going to be his last day. I just came in, and of course everybody left us alone in the room like they normally do, and they turned off the baby monitor. I sat down and was holding his hand. You always wish there was more you could say."

Sue's voice cracks, and she begins to cry.

> "I told him that I would take care of everything. You could almost see him just relax at that point. I said to him, "Gene, you are always saying, 'Let's get on with it.' It's time to get on with it. I will take care of Joanie. I kissed him on his bald little head and told him I loved him.
>
> "That was probably about three o'clock in the afternoon. I think that you could see that he relaxed and was ready at that point. I had gone into the kitchen and was talking to everybody in there for a little while. Ann was with him to see if there was anything she could do to make him

more comfortable. And then she came out and said, 'I think you need to come in.'

"I came in and I sat down. All the volunteers were there, sitting at the foot of the bed. He was sleeping, and he looked so peaceful. You know, the weird thing about it is that he looked healthier at that point than he had in his whole illness. His skin was clear; he looked relaxed; he looked really healthy, other than the fact that he was yellow.

"He didn't have to worry about anything anymore, knowing that Joanie was going to be taken care of. That probably had a lot to do with how he looked.

"His passing was an absolutely beautiful exit for him. Gene's whole life, from high school through his retirement, was all spent in theater—you know, putting on plays, acting in plays, producing, being an artistic director, managing theaters...the whole thing. He had always been in the arts and in the theater.

"So here he was, almost on a stage, with all of us there trying to help him. He didn't just pass; he didn't just quietly go in his sleep. I happened to look over, and I saw something different in his face.

"His eyes were trying to open, and all of a sudden his eyes did open, and he was focused. He turned his head, and he looked directly into my face. Of course, he didn't say anything. He just looked at me like he wanted me to know something. When he looked at me, I waved at the other people to come. They all got up and came over and stood next to the bed. He turned his face and looked right at them, and then he looked at me. He rolled his head to one side, closed his eyes, took two breaths, and then he was gone.

"Ann said, 'Oh my God. That was incredible.' She is so great. She stood up and started clapping and saying, 'Bravo, Gene!' Everybody else started doing it too. 'Bravo, Gene, you did it!'

"His whole life was that way. He got a standing ovation from them. And then I turned and I said, 'Open the window! Quick, open the window!' So we opened the window.

"MyoO lit a candle. Ann opened a bottle of champagne and poured Gene a glass and then poured champagne for everybody else. We all just watched and said, 'Bravo, Gene, you did it exactly the way you should have.'"

Michael

Pam's husband, Michael, came to Enso House shortly before his sixty-ninth birthday. Having been diagnosed with lung cancer, Michael had surgery to remove part of his lung, but doctors discovered that he had a rare, very fast-growing, aggressive cancer that resulted in a large production of mucus. Doctors said his cancer was incurable but could be slowed with treatment. He had four rounds of chemotherapy; each treatment left him bedridden for another ten days.

Six months into treatment, Michael needed to have part of his colon removed and an ileostomy—part of his small intestine routed outside his body. During his recovery from that surgery, they discovered that his cancer had continued to progress. Doctors told Michael and Pam about a new experimental drug that might help. They tried that, but Michael had a strong toxic reaction to the first dose. They tried a different combination, but he had a bad reaction to that too. Doctors found an embolism in his lungs.

The morning following admittance to the hospital, Michael told Pam, "Take me out of here. I want to go home. I want to die at home."

Pam ordered all medical treatment to be stopped, and contacted a hospice. She and other family members began taking care of Michael at home while a hospice nurse visited twice a week. The hospice nurse administered Lorazepam orally for treating anxiety, and morphine for pain. Eventually, Michael needed it once an hour and had great difficulty swallowing. It took fifteen minutes to administer the medication; then forty-five minutes later, around the clock, he needed another dose. Pam, her three children, and their partners all helped, each taking a three-hour shift throughout the day. After a few weeks, Pam was exhausted.

"I hit bottom. I remember getting out of bed and starting my duty, walking through the room, and feeling like I weighed five hundred pounds, just dragging my feet, not seeing anything in front of me, and getting to the threshold of the family room where we had set up Mike in a hospital bed, and saying, 'I just cannot do this anymore.' My kids were all there, and they said, 'Good, good—we have been waiting for you to be able to back out and just be his wife, Mom.'

"They were all nervous about how they were going to proceed without me, but they knew how to do it, so I just crapped out for two days. I could hardly move. And then each day, one of the kids hit the wall. The next day the oldest one, and the next day the other one; the next day the younger one; and their partners were supportive but exhausted. So we just started thinking about, what can we do? We couldn't think of anything. We had utilized all of our friends. They were all there; they were all helping, but it was just too overwhelming.

Pam herself was a trained caregiver specialist. She had spent the last ten years conducting workshops, leading training groups, and counseling caregivers. She had worked to help people understand the importance for caregivers to take care of themselves.

"But until you actually do it, until you are actually in the trenches living every moment as the caregiver, you can't know the intensity of it. It's the nuances; it's the subtleties; it's got so many layers; it's not simple anymore. Every decision I made—even when to go to the bathroom—was based on him at that moment, not anything else, not even my most basic needs. Additionally, there was the responsibility of coordinating the other helpers. It was just unbelievable. Just thinking about it now, I am overwhelmed."

Years earlier Pam had heard about Enso House through the quarterly caregiver retreats offered at the monastery. She says,

"I brought some caregivers over here once, and while the retreat was going on at the monastery, I walked over to Enso House, and I met Ann. Walking in the door was like, 'Oh my God! What this place has to offer is unbelievable.' I observed someone sitting with a guest, and it was just beautiful. I referred the place often."

Now she was searching for an alternative way to care for Michael.

"On a Tuesday morning, I woke up and went from my bed to my table where I sit and have my coffee with Michael every morning. And Enso House just came to my mind. I looked at my watch, and it was about ten minutes until eight. So I just sat for a few minutes, and then as soon as I could, I made the call, and Ann answered the phone."

Ann went over to Seattle to meet Michael. It turned out that when Ann showed up, his chaplain and hospice nurses were there as well. Pam remembers,

"Ann was very gentle and professional. She sat at Mike's bedside and introduced herself and her purpose for being there. She mentioned that I had called and that we were all just exhausted. I cannot remember all the details, but she said, 'So what do you think?' and Michael said, 'Well, I don't want to offend anybody or break any trust, but I have felt cheated.' Ann said, 'What do you mean?' And he said, 'Well, I always wanted to go to a hospice place if I had the choice.' I was dumbfounded. This was the first time I had heard of it. With all of my talking with him about hospice, we never once referred to a place to do it. Because I thought to do it at home was the ideal. So when he said a hospice place, it was like hallelujah!

"Historically, Mike doesn't like change; he has difficulty making transitions, but he was so open to hearing about Enso House. I was blown away. The kids were in the other room, and they heard him on the baby monitor. They said that their jaws just dropped. They didn't expect him to want to go. Before Ann left, she talked to the doctor, his oncologist. She talked with a social worker and with a Whidbey General hospice nurse. Things were set in motion, and she said,

'The soonest we could get him in there is Tuesday'. That was only one day away."

"The next day, I was the happiest person in the world. The man I loved was going to get his wish. And we were going to get some help without having to abandon our hopes for his final days. Nothing was going to worry me, but sure enough, as the day progressed, each hour that we had to administer the medicine, it was like, 'Don't die now Mike; don't die now.' When the ambulance came, we were prepared, and it was an effortless drive.

"He was on a gurney, and when we went through the front door and we came into the main room and the light shining through the windows was a gorgeous honey hue—I mean, it was like a huge honey pot. And his little blue eyes just sparkled, and he grinned from ear to ear, and he said, 'Oh, I feel like I am home.'

"Ann and MyoO situated the bed, so it was facing out where he could see the birdfeeder and the pasture and the trees, the pond and the whole vista. It was just lovely, beautiful. Eventually, everybody left and we began to settle in. It felt like we were at a lodge, a lodge where everything was at our disposal, and this was going to be, in my estimation, our final vacation, our last road trip."

Almost immediately, Ann began assessing his situation and was able to order fentanyl transdermal patches for Michael, which meant he would receive his painkiller medication through the skin and would no longer have to swallow pills every hour. This was a huge benefit for Michael and a huge relief for Pam and his children, who had witnessed his struggle with the medications to that point.

Within days, some psychological issues began to surface. Pam recalls,

> "I think we had come to appreciate the frustrations he was feeling. When he was at home, he wanted to go away to a hospice. Once he got here, he wanted to go back home. He seemed agitated and angry, suspicious and paranoid. With Ann's help, we recognized that it is not uncommon for people to want out of their situation. But they cannot say it; they just want out. They don't want to be in this situation; they don't want to die. They don't want to do this thing called dying.

> "So wherever they are, they're going to most likely resist. And that was fine. He could do it here. He wasn't shamed or bribed or cajoled. Everyone understood what he was talking about. We continually affirmed him. And he eventually understood."

Michael felt most comfortable when his care was managed by people he saw as "professionals." Dr. Ann Cutcher, however, had always presented herself with humility and had shunned the formalities that might separate her as an authority. Following Pam's request,

Ann attempted to speak with a more authoritative voice. She found her white coat and name tag, and put her stethoscope around her neck. These simple acts were all that Michael needed. Michael passed away three weeks after coming to Enso House. Pam was full of gratitude.

> "Being here was Mike's last gift to us. I was able to be with him those last few days in a way that was just amazing and extremely intimate. It was a real blessing to be with him and not have to be anywhere else. The world was right, and everything was going on as it should. The kids were able to move back to their own homes and be busy doing their own things, living their own lives, knowing their dad was in the best place possible.

> "I had to thank Enso House and all the people who support it. Every neighborhood should have one. And we were so blessed to be able to be there."

Jane

I am sitting in Susan Tomic's office listening to her story about her dear friend and partner, Jane. Susan has a framed sign on the wall saying, "Only love and no fear."

Jane was born in a highly regarded family in New York City. Her father was an interior designer and antique collector. Her mother was a ballet dancer who trained dancers for the New York City Ballet. She then moved to Seattle to become the first director of the Pacific Northwest Ballet. Jane was bright, energetic and attractive, ten years younger than her brother Reed. At the age of 28, her friends started calling her "Jane the Brain" after she won a championship on the TV show *Jeopardy!* She had musical talent and played electric bass in a series of rock bands. In 1992 she started one of the first Pilates studios in Seattle and trained many instructors in the Pacific Northwest. She was always health conscious; she loved to eat organic food and got plenty of exercise. Jane always had a great sense of humor, a quick wit and an easy smile.

Throughout her adult life, Jane formed intimate relationships with women, including a long-term relationship with Donna, a woman with a two-year old daughter, Marina. Jane and Donna shared parental responsibilities for sixteen years. Eventually the two women separated, and one of the unfortunate consequences was an emotional rift between Jane and her stepdaughter, Marina.

Later, Jane met Susan. The two bonded quickly and established a strong and loving partnership. Susan had her own daughter, Chelsea, who became Jane's second stepdaughter. Jane and Susan went into business together, establishing a company, New Earth Neurocare, which used a brain training technology to help people develop greater clarity in their lives.

At the age of fifty-four, Jane was at the peak of her career and apparently in excellent health. In February 2012, the two entrepreneurs were preparing to go to a neuro-feedback conference when Jane was suddenly struck by severe pain in her abdomen. Susan took her to Whidbey General Hospital for emergency care where doctors discovered severe internal bleeding. After receiving a blood transfusion, she was airlifted to Harborview Medical Center in Seattle where doctors were able to stop the bleeding. She had lost nearly half her blood volume into her abdominal cavity. Unfortunately, because blood is opaque to certain imaging systems, it was impossible to ascertain the cause of the bleeding. Doctors had to wait until the blood had cleared out. Jane suffered a series of pain crises and returned to the emergency room seventeen times over the next few months.

Surgery was scheduled two months later for what was believed to be a benign tumor—cancerous tumors don't usually cause hemorrhaging. Surgeons discovered a tumor on her liver that had caused a blood vessel to break. In fact they found not one, but many cancerous tumors. It was melanoma, but doctors could find no primary tumor. The prognosis was grim. Doctors told Jane that there was nothing more they could do for her. They suggested that she go home and get her affairs in order.

But Susan and Jane were both determined to fight the disease using naturopathic methods. They began with a

Gerson Therapy diet: vegetarian food, raw juices, coffee enemas and natural supplements. Jane took baths with hydrogen peroxide and had saunas with infrared lamps. She stopped eating sugar. After another pain crisis, Jane was taken to the emergency room again and had a CT scan. Doctors discovered that her tumors had grown to the size of baseballs. In desperation, Jane began an unconventional therapy program involving intravenous "essential nutrients" for five hours a day, five days a week. She tried to down nearly 30 pills a day. Unfortunately, the tumors had grown so large that her digestive system was blocked. Even keeping down a half cup of soup was impossible.

One day when Susan went to pick Jane up at the clinic, it was raining. Jane came out in her raincoat, fell to the ground on one knee in the mud, and vomited onto the pavement. Susan took her to the emergency room again. Another CT scan showed that the tumors were huge. Susan said to Jane, "Look, you are terminal. You are going to die. We need to turn and face death. You need to spend your life, the rest of what you have, in a way that is life-giving, saying farewell to your friends and family, instead of pursuing this stuff."

With the guidance of staff from Whidbey Home Health Care & Hospice, Jane's treatment was redirected toward palliative care. Jane had grown severely malnourished but wanted to be able to say goodbye to friends and family around the world. Using a port that had been implanted into her chest, she began a regimen of intravenous nutrition or TPN (Total Parenteral Nutrition). TPN is sometimes indicated for patients who cannot absorb nutrients through their gut. In Jane's case, her stomach was completely blocked by the large tumors. The TPN provided the energy she needed to tide her over for a few weeks as she contacted friends via email, Facebook and Skype. Susan continued the complex task of administering the medications needed to keep Jane's pain under control.

Even at this late stage in Jane's illness, it was hard for her to accept that she was dying. Without Jane's knowledge, Susan contacted Enso House. She was attracted to the spiritual aspects, something which had been missing so far in her efforts to deal with Jane's dying. She called Ann to discuss their options. After one conversation, when Susan hung up the phone, Jane asked her, "Was that Enso House?" Susan said, "Yes, but how did you know that I called Enso House?" Jane said, "Well, I was thinking about them." Susan was stunned. This was a key turning point. Susan said that she had already made an appointment and asked Jane if she wanted to go see it. Jane agreed.

Jane met Ann and picked the room she liked which overlooked the pasture. However, it was not quite the right time for her admission. Ann explained that continuing the TPN regimen at Enso House would not be appropriate. To be admitted to Enso House, a guest needs to be ready to die and shift away from treatments for extending life toward pain management and comfort care. As a person is dying, TPN becomes more of a burden than an asset. The body is in decline and cannot metabolize the nutrients or process the extra fluid. The belly becomes distended and fluid collects in the legs, resulting in greater suffering.

Remembering the visit, Susan says, "We were very happy about the situation. It was a very peaceful place. It felt like home. They were preparing food. It was in the country. It was perfect." They knew that the next step was now in place. In the meantime, Jane was able to continue seeing visitors and saying her goodbyes.

Jane's best friend from high school showed up from New York and walked into Jane's bedroom. Jane opened her eyes, had instant recognition and greeted her old friend with open arms. Her brother, Reed, whom she hadn't seen for several years, flew in from Spain. Jane's stepdaughter, Marina, came from Italy where she is an aspiring circus performer. She and Jane had been estranged for many years, but now there was an opportunity for changing their relationship.

Day by day Jane's condition continued to worsen. Her body was emaciated. A protruding belly grew larger every day. It was time to discontinue TPN. It was time to say goodbye to her home, her dog and cat, and her familiar surroundings. It was time to walk down the stairs, get into the car and drive away, knowing that she would never come back. It was time to go to Enso House. Jane told Susan, "There is no longer room for me to live in my body. I cannot laugh in my body. I cannot cry in my body. There is no room for the tumor and me so I have to leave."

When they arrived at Enso House, Susan got out of the car and started walking around to help Jane get out. But Jane got out herself and walked unassisted. Following right behind her were Susan, Chelsea, Reed, and Marina. Jane came in the front door and walked directly to the room she had selected. She plopped down on the bed and said, "I'm here. Let's get on with it."

Everyone in the family expected that Jane had only a few days left. They brought air mattresses along for sleeping on the floor.

Susan remembers that she had never discussed with Ann the possibility of the whole family moving in. She knew that the daily rate was $145, but she did not realize that this would include three meals a day for everyone. She was impressed that Enso House staff members were totally welcoming. Even the family dog, Tasha, was welcomed for visits. Susan appreciated that she could bring a favorite bottle of single malt scotch for sharing with friends. Her reception at Enso House was in stark contrast to what she had experienced in institutional settings where "you get so lost in the paperwork and the liability and the insurance cards and everything that you are robbed of the fertile emotional experiences. Here at Enso House, there was none of that—nothing other than welcoming. It was amazing."

Finally, Jane was settled in at Enso House. Assisting Ann and MyoO as one of the core caregivers was Kozan (Piotr Roszczenko), a young man in his mid-twenties, one of Shodo Harada's students at Sogenji. While this was his first close experience with the dying process, Kozan put himself wholeheartedly into support mode and helped in every way he could.

Before coming together at Enso House, relationships between Jane and Reed and Marina had been strained. Susan's sixteen-year-old daughter, Chelsea, had not met them before, but after being together for a week, these people became a makeshift family. Reed composed poetry for his sister. Chelsea helped with the caregiving. At night, Marina spent time in the bed embracing Jane. During the day, she did cartwheels and handstands on the living room floor.

Susan asked Jane if she wanted to see Donna, her former wife and Marina's mother. Her relationship with Jane had been severely strained, so the opportunity for Donna and Jane to see each other offered the opportunity for tremendous healing. Jane said, "Yes, I would like to see her." So Donna came to visit. The meeting turned into a 10-hour marathon of laughter and silliness. Seeing so many old friends, reuniting with relatives and finding reconciliation of strained relationships with others put Jane in a state of bliss. Susan says, "When she finally turned to embrace death, she did it wholeheartedly. By the time she left, there was very little luggage that she took with her. When people came to visit her, they left with more than what they gave. Jane was radiating. She was absolutely beautiful—especially here at Enso House. It wasn't the activities that caused the bliss; it was the embracing of death. That is what was elevating her spirit."

The pain of Jane's illness became more and more difficult. One night, she was escorted in a wheelchair to the bathroom. After getting up from the wheelchair she was completely out of breath and had trouble breathing all night. While it seemed to the family that Jane might die that night, Ann explained that the feeling of being unable to breathe was not unusual and that Jane still had a lot of life left in her. Seven days after coming to Enso House, Jane was still very much alive. At this point, visitors began to leave, one by one. Marina returned to Italy; Reed returned to Spain. Chelsea left for a pre-planned trip to Europe. All three were very tearful. Jane was alone with Susan and told her, "I am finally alone with you and all I want to do is be with you, and I am too stupid to even put a sentence together."

After having taken no food for seven days, Jane said to Ann, "What can I do? What can I do to get out of this body? You have to help me." Ann said, "You need to stop drinking water. That's the only thing you have control of."

Susan was intent on helping Jane to make her death a conscious one. A spiritual group associated with Indian gurus Sri Amma Bhagavan came to give their blessings to Jane. Recordings of Hindu hymns were played throughout the day. An a cappella singing group came and a harpist provided soothing music. It had been nearly three weeks with no food and one week with no water. It was amazing to everyone that Jane was still alive.

Each morning, Susan and Jane would say a prayer, "Please fill us today with so much divine grace that there is no room left for fear." They were both surprised that Jane was still alive. Jane could no longer sleep, but shifted restlessly throughout the night. Both of them grew more anxious. Susan said, "We kept trying to soothe our anxiety with the idea that this was a blessed process. Much like pregnancy, it is like you are on the conveyor belt of life and there is no getting off. I remember feeling that when I was pregnant. It was a life force kind of process where you no longer had control of your body. This was like the same thing. You are waiting for the gestation process of death. It is the ultimate test of letting go."

This high level of expectation reminded Kozan of Zen practice at Sogenji: "It was really interesting how long the process took. It can go on and on. It reminded me of the way people are in sanzen, wanting some breakthrough to happen, and pressing Roshi, "How long will this take? What is supposed to happen?" But the process continues on its own. It has its own timing."

Susan lay beside Jane, stroked her arm and whispered, "Your lungs served you well all your life, but you don't need them where you're going now. Your heart served you well, but you don't need it anymore. There's nothing to fear. There is only love."

One morning, Jane declared, "Get me the hell out of here. I want to die." What more could be done for her? Now, ten days after being admitted to Enso House, Jane was on the verge of losing consciousness. Ann was prepared to increase Jane's dosage of anti-anxiety medication which could precipitate further loss of consciousness.

Susan struggled. At this point, she and Jane had not been able to say goodbye to each other. She wanted Jane to find relief, but was afraid that after an increase in medication, she would never be able to actually say goodbye.

After the medication was administered, Susan tried to communicate with Jane on a non-physical plane. She tried dripping hot oil on her own forehead—an ancient ayurvedic technique used to open the "third eye".

Silently, Susan spoke to Jane: "Soon you will be seeing your father, your mother, your pets. It would be a good time to forgive your father, because you will be seeing him shortly. Let's practice walking to the veil together. Let's practice leaving your body."

Soon Jane's breathing became more rapid, labored and noisy, the distinctive gurgling sound known as the death rattle that generally indicates death is imminent. For Jane, this stage continued for an unusually long time—nearly twelve hours. Susan couldn't understand why Jane's dying process was taking so long: "She has said goodbye to everybody. What could she possibly be waiting for?"

Then a psychic was called in. Sizing up the situation, the psychic said, 'Jane is still waiting for something.' At that point, Kozan went out to check the mail. There was a letter for Jane sent in care of Enso House. Susan read the letter to her. It was from another one of her ex-wives, a very loving letter with a heart-felt apology.

Jane drifted into a completely non-responsive state; she seemed unconscious. Then suddenly Jane opened her eyes, looked directly at Susan and said clearly, "I have to go now. Goodbye honey. I will see you soon."

Then a friend of Susan's showed up. Susan declared that she had had enough of this "somber shit," and decided to lighten things up a bit. Jane used to love singing and dancing to Motown music, so Susan got out the bottle of scotch to share with her friend, fired up her computer and started playing Jane's favorite songs, beginning with Marvin Gaye's, "I Heard it Through the

Grapevine." A party atmosphere ensued. But the anxiety level continued to grow, among everyone, including Jane.

The fluid in Jane's lungs was severely interfering with her breathing. The upper third of her bed was elevated so Jane was nearly upright. Suddenly, according to Kozan, "All hell broke loose." Fluids started coming up and were being forcefully expelled from Jane's lungs. Apparently, one of the tumors had burst, releasing large quantities of pus and phlegm. Ann and Kozan quickly set up a medical suction device to vacuum up material from her mouth and throat. It was a task that went on for hours: aspirating her mouth, emptying material from the aspirator, wiping up with towels and tissues, trying to keep up with this surprising new development in the dying process.

The death rattle breathing was incessant, punctuated by violent expulsions of fluid. Before this started, this had been the smoothest, most beautiful, most blessed death that Ann had seen. The end was gruesome. Kozan felt that Jane's personality or spirit was gone after she lost 'ordinary consciousness.' Her face was a non-emotive mask. The process he witnessed seemed to be happening to a body, not a person.

Jane's dosage of the painkiller Dilaudid, delivered intravenously, was at its maximum level. This was the most effective way to help her breathe easier but a side effect, at this dosage is to eventually cause death.

Jane's body was still exhibiting rhythmic convulsions while she was held sitting up against the raised bed. Lowering the head of the bed might bring the process to a close more quickly. Was it more compassionate to keep her sitting up or to let her lie down and rest? As Susan lowered the bed, she whispered in Jane's ear, "Only love and no fear. Only love and no fear." Lying down, Jane passed away within about five minutes. The struggle was over.

Everyone sat down and took a deep breath. Not only had Jane's brain ceased functioning; every person in the room was experiencing a moment of profound quiet. All the impatience, all the agonizing, all the struggling had ceased. Medical explanations, spiritual strivings, opinions of right and wrong—none of this mattered. Nothing remained but an amazing sense of intimacy.

Dairin at the monastery was called. He came over, stood beside Jane's body, rang a bell and led chanting of the Heart Sutra and the Song of Zazen. Susan remembers this as "resoundingly beautiful and reverent. It was perfect." She appreciated the intentional slowing of the process, saying prayers, and sitting quietly with the body.

Ann led a process of washing the body. Just then, two of Jane's friends showed up and without a bit of hesitation, joined in what felt like an important sacred ceremony. The water was taken out to the garden and used to water the plants. After the body was washed, Jane was dressed with the clothes she had selected. In honor of her fondest memories as bass player in a rock band, Jane had chosen her silver lamé smoking jacket and leopard skin pointed toe boots. Her body rested in the bed overnight while Enso House prepared a meal for everyone. To Susan, this felt like the most normalizing thing she could have imagined. "It was like you finished a marathon. The body was lying 10 feet from us as we were sitting around the dining room table, having a simple, beautiful dinner with whole foods. It was so healing. Sharing a meal was such a normalization, after the horrific process that had just ended."

Dry ice was obtained from the fish department at the Payless grocery and placed under the body to keep it cool. A friend who worked in construction had made a simple pine box casket. The next day, he arrived with his van and transported the body back to Jane's home.

To make a body presentable for a wake, the eyes and mouth must be closed before rigor mortis sets in. Coins were placed on Jane's eyelids to hold them down, but her eyelids kept popping open. Fortunately the construction worker friend had some heavier large washers in his truck that did the trick. Keeping the mouth closed was also a challenge but Susan and her friend Marti found a plaid scarf to tie around the head to hold the jaw shut. Susan put makeup on Jane's face and prepared her hair with dry shampoo to prepare the body for the wake.

Describing the evening, Susan said, "I slept in the bed with Jane and I had a very deep sleep. I didn't feel awkward at all. It just felt so good to not have somebody whisk her away. To just rest. I had a very restful evening. There wasn't anybody pushing the process along." She continues,

> "It is so amazing. I was raised a Catholic and I never understood the open casket thing. But I get it now. It's very important to register in your psyche that this is the body that looks like Jane, but Jane's not here. Therefore the spirit has moved on and there is a separation of the two—spirit and body. When you see the lack of animation in a dead body, when you see the lifelessness and the lack of spirit, it really helps to understand that the spirit continues to live on."

Susan had researched the legal requirements and worked with county and state officials to learn how to do the things that a funeral director normally does: transporting a body, displaying a body in an open casket, delivering a body to the crematorium. Susan got certified copies of a death certificate from Jane's doctor and took these to the county office where she obtained a body transport permit.

Susan said, "The next morning, my friend, Pat, showed up with his tinker van full of tools, with a beer in his hand, and we gurneyed her out to the van. It was like an old Irish wake."

Susan's sister, Nancy, arrived from New York and joined her in preparing for the wake. They brought Jane's body to the home and put her into a simple casket lined with silk and pillows. Flowers, cards, pictures and music were carefully arranged to present a beautiful setting. Jane's friends were invited to pay their respects during a twenty-four hour vigil.

> "The first visitor was here before Nancy and I
> woke up in the morning but everything was
> open here and she came in before work. She is a
> free-form dance person and she said it was so
> beautiful—she just danced around the body.
> Then she left and went to work. So we had
> people all day long until 10 o'clock at night."

Susan and Nancy arranged to take Jane's body to a special crematorium where family members are allowed to accompany the body and witness the cremation.

When they arrived at the crematorium, the three women transferred the casket out of the car and onto rollers. They paused to bless the body with holy water and frankincense. Then they rolled the casket into the oven, closed the door and turned on the oven. During the process, Jane's body was accompanied at all times by those who loved her.

Susan was grateful that they had been able to do their own funeral:

> "She was not whisked away to a funeral home. She wasn't put in a refrigerator overnight. She didn't reappear with all of her blood gone, replaced with formaldehyde. She didn't look perfect with the makeup and the hair. And the whole thing, casket included was maybe $3,000, versus $15,000 if you do it with a funeral home. That word *reverence* just keeps coming to me when I talk about this because it was just so intimate.

> "So then we drove immediately to Thirteen Coins and ordered a bottle of champagne. We had some orange juice and entered into an altered state. I really couldn't believe that I had just put my wife into an oven."

DEATH WITH DIGNITY

*Our further prayer is not to be extremely ill or to
be suffering at the time of departure, to know its
coming seven days ahead, so that we can quiet the
mind to abandon the body and be unattached to all
things at the last moment, wherein we return to
the Original Mind in the realm of no birth and no
death and merge infinitely into the whole universe,
to manifest as all things in their True Nature.*

—*Dai E Zenji*[19]

In 2008, voters in Washington State, by a majority
of 57.8 percent, approved a measure to allow
terminally ill patients to determine the time of their
own death by ingesting a lethal dosage of medication. It
wasn't long before the question came to Enso House:
What to do if a guest wished to be involved in the Death
with Dignity program?

In 2009, a young man afflicted with throat cancer, who
was being cared for by his brother, a lay Buddhist
monk, came to Enso House seeking admission. The
man had seen two physicians, each of whom
determined that he had less than six months to live.
Facing the prospect of becoming unable to swallow and
choking on his own blood, he had obtained from a
pharmacy the medication that could end his life.

Ann, the physician who oversees medical care at Enso House, knew that board members had different points of view about the Death with Dignity law. She realized that these differences had been neither discussed among themselves, nor with Roshi. She told the young man that we were unable to accept him right away because we needed to discuss his particular circumstances with the board first.

Our board of directors includes Roshi and Chisan, Charles and Betsy, George Moseley, Ed, Patty, Taigan, Cynthia, and me. At this point we realized that several of us held strong opinions about this issue, that our points of view differed significantly, that the issue was highly charged politically, that it could have a big impact on our reputation in the community, and finally, that we didn't know how Roshi would advise us on the issue. It seemed that this issue might result in a rift among board members. In a worst-case scenario, it was possible that things could spiral out of control and that Enso House would no longer be able to function as it had.

Modeled after an Oregon law that has been in place since 1997, the Death with Dignity provision requires evidence of mental competency and a diagnosis of terminal illness with less than six months to live as verified by two physicians. The patient must be informed of all other options, including palliative and hospice care. They must make two voluntary requests, without coercion, also verified by two physicians. In addition, there are waiting periods specified between making an oral request, submitting a written request, and having the prescription filled; the patient may change his or her mind at any time and rescind the request.

When the Death with Dignity initiative appeared on the ballot in 2008, I voted for it. My view was that if one wants to plan the timing of one's own death, then that is each person's prerogative.

In grappling with these questions, I have tried to put myself in the situation of being within weeks or months of the end of my life. I can imagine terminal conditions that would cause me to choke to death or enter a coma for an indefinite period or lose all brain functioning—situations in which I believe dying by way of a lethal medication would be preferable. Granted, it is not necessarily possible for anyone to die according to a plan; nevertheless, I do feel that I have a right to influence how I die.

Some board members had voted for the initiative, and others had voted against it. Each of us had to ask ourselves, "How should we think about this?" Is it suicide? Euthanasia? Is it an act of individual freedom? Can this be decided strictly as an individual? Does the community have an interest in how an individual dies? Is there the danger of a "slippery slope," whereby people who are merely inconvenient to have around (who are seen that way or who see themselves that way) begin pursuing this option for the wrong reasons? One board member, whose uncle had committed suicide, strongly opposed any actions or legislation that supported suicide in any way.

To me, it is clear that as individuals, we can and do make decisions that shorten our lives: with a terminal diagnosis of cancer, we can refuse to have another round of chemotherapy. With kidney disease, we can decide to terminate dialysis. As we approach death, we can stop eating and drinking. It is also clear that we frequently take actions sanctioned by society that shorten the lives of others: in hospitals and nursing homes, it is not uncommon to increase dosages of painkiller narcotics, knowing full well that doing so both reduces pain and hastens death.

Aside from these intellectual ruminations, however, the most compelling reason I believe in the right to die comes from stories told by people who have chosen Death with Dignity. One of those people was Ethan Remmel, Associate Professor at Western Washington University, who was terminally ill and decided to obtain the drug that could legally end his life. He recorded his experiences in a blog on the *Psychology Today* website[20]. When he obtained the drug, Ethan explained that while he had not yet decided whether to use it, he had comfort in knowing that he had some control of his dying process. He wrote,

"I do not think of using the medication as suicide, and I don't think others should either. It would be part of a dying process that has already begun, not of my choice."

Ethan expressed a sense of responsibility to share his experience with the world to contribute to the discussion and address the stigma associated with the Death with Dignity Law. As Ethan's condition worsened, he eventually chose to take the drug and died on June 13, 2011.

Reflecting on Ethan's story, I easily identify with his need to make his own choices about how much pain to bear and when to call it quits. The value of choice near the end of life continues to inform my involvement in end-of-life care.

I soon realized that my point of view differed not only from those of some board members but from my teacher, Shodo Harada Roshi, as well. In a meeting at Sogenji to address the issue, Roshi stated, "Death with Dignity seems to me to be basically suicide." He referred to the first of Bodhidharma's One Mind precepts that says, "From the most clear, profound, and subtle mind, to not kill life."

Roshi emphasized the fundamental perspective that living beings are not separate from one another, but exist as part of a universal whole: our choices cannot be made independently of society or separate from other people. Roshi underscored the importance of improving our care of people who are dying; doing so would make it unnecessary to consider Death with Dignity.

Ed Lorah is President of the board of directors at Enso House. He has worked with end-of-life concerns since 1992 as a hospice social worker. Most recently, Ed has been working to help doctors understand the new law and how it relates to patients who want to be in control of ending their own lives.

Ed wondered how his new responsibilities might affect his relationship with Enso House or his relationship with Roshi. He says,

> "I realized quickly that the Roshi and I had a
> fundamental difference in the way that we
> looked at things. The culture here is very
> different."

Ed met with the Roshi in an effort to resolve the discrepancy between Ed's beliefs about his work and the Roshi's statements about Death with Dignity. In the meeting, Roshi did not tell Ed what to do, but expressed trust in Ed's own judgment.

I felt that my own feelings were close to those of Ed. One of the things I was most concerned about was making a public declaration of Enso House policy. If we said we supported Death with Dignity, then we risked the very real possibility of attack and bad publicity about Enso House. On the other hand, if we declared that we opposed Death with Dignity, then in effect we would be turning our backs on people who wanted to have some control over how they die. How could our expression of compassion for all people be compatible with refusing out of hand those who would consider obtaining, legally, medication for ending their life? I realized that I felt strongly about this; if it came down to the board declaring that we would refuse to admit anyone who was considering this option, then I was prepared to withdraw my support for Enso House.

I could also see quite clearly how damaging it would be for Enso House to be seen as "the place to go" to take lethal medications. The whole point of Enso House is to provide care and comfort to patients while the dying process progresses in a natural way. Others on the board agreed that it was unnecessary to make a public declaration one way or the other. We did reach consensus that Ann should continue to use her best judgment in deciding which prospective patients had the best fit with the Enso House mission.

It is not uncommon, among patients in Oregon and Washington who have obtained the lethal medication, to not actually take the drugs before they die. In Oregon from 1994 to 2011, 935 people had prescriptions for lethal medication through Death with Dignity, and 596 patients died from ingesting it.[21] This means that 36 percent never used the medication. Sometimes, the motivation for obtaining the medication is the fear of not having access to palliative care at the end of life or the fear of losing control. In some cases, having access to palliative care with appropriate medication for pain and anxiety obviates the need to take the lethal drugs.

In February 2010, at a public talk on Whidbey Island, Roshi spoke again about the Death with Dignity Act. It seemed to me that Roshi's position had softened a bit. He acknowledged that there could indeed be certain extreme situations in which a person's pain is so severe and intractable that a doctor might feel it necessary to treat the pain with strong medication that may have a side effect of bringing the patient's life to a close more quickly. However, he also raised concerns about situations where there may be other motivations for speeding death.

For example, he pointed out that elderly people generally do not want to be a burden to their children. If children were to encourage a parent to take lethal medication, the parent might agree to do so, even before they are close to dying naturally. Roshi also talked about older people who no longer live in a close and intimate family situation but are living by themselves with no one to share meals with and no one to talk to about problems they are going through. Living lonely lives by themselves, they may be only too ready to end their lives.

Michael Lerner, President of Commonweal and a friend of Roshi's, in his work with cancer patients, has met many people who are facing imminent death. He describes the dilemma of the Death with Dignity initiative.

"This is one of those many matters where there are very profound truths on both sides of an issue. It's not that one side is right and the other side is wrong. Roshi's perspective here is based on a very profound spiritual insight. It is analogous to the insight that conception of human life is sacred. I think that when these issues encounter each other, the way to find the best healing is to honor both sides equally and not to dismiss a perspective based on spiritual insight just because, in this moment, it is culturally unpopular.

"Many of the Catholic perceptions about end-of-life apply here. The people who oppose these laws, as Roshi does and as the Catholics do, have very important points. One is that this right to a good death is a very slippery slope. Once you start granting people the capacity to choose euthanasia or assisted suicide, or whatever you want to call it, I can tell you that there are many older people who do not want to be a burden to their families in their older age and do not want to burn through their savings and leave their families nothing. People may perceive that their families see them as a burden or that they are no longer valued because they can no longer contribute.

"As this becomes enshrined in the culture, it becomes easier and easier for people to decide that they are an economic burden, they are an emotional burden, their children don't have time for them, so on and so forth, so they may decide it's time to check out.

"Also, with cancer, specifically, depression often accompanies a cancer diagnosis. What I am pointing to is that this is not an easy shot. This is not something where the people who feel, as I feel, that these laws are important and helpful have any clear spiritual superiority or ethical or moral superiority to those on the other side of the argument. I just believe that this issue should be treated with the greatest and most tender respect on both sides."

The young man who originally approached Enso House with the question of Death with Dignity found a place with his sister to continue his convalescence. A community of friends and neighbors cared for him, and he lived for another year. Then finally, he collapsed and his brother took him to the hospital. His brother called Ann and asked if he could be admitted. Ann said, "Yes, of course."

Then all of a sudden, a major blood vessel burst, and the man died quickly from internal bleeding. He never took the lethal medication.

Since then, Ann has received a couple of calls about people considering the Death with Dignity option. For example, she heard from a social worker at the hospital in Port Townsend who was developing a discharge plan for a patient who had been in the Death with Dignity program. She asked Ann, "Do you participate in the Death with Dignity program?" Ann replied, "We have made the decision not to directly participate, but if someone chose to do that once they were here, we would do our best to find an appropriate place for them to be—which is at home." Ann says,

> "So there were maybe a couple of phone calls asking if we participated. And it was easy for me to say, 'No, we don't actively participate.' And that keeps it simple. That really keeps it simple. I just remember hearing the Roshi say, 'Keep it simple.'"

Reflecting on my own point of view, I think there has been some evolution. I still believe that people with a terminal illness should have the right to choose how and when they die. It is not my place to tell anyone what they should or shouldn't do at this most precious time of their life. But I also believe that it is not necessary for Enso House to participate in the Death with Dignity program. Specifically, having Enso House staff members witness patients ingesting lethal drugs does not seem to me consistent with our mission of palliative care. When it comes down to the final days of someone's life, the best we can do is to simply be with that person, letting go of our plans and expectations, and experience this mysterious process together.

This then seems to me the best policy: we don't necessarily refuse anyone who has begun the Death with Dignity process, including obtaining lethal medication, but we also do not participate in guests taking these medications on the premises. Instead, we continue what have always done: providing the best possible care we are capable of giving, comforting and holding the hand of the guest as death progresses at its own pace.

Zen Training and Death

Let me respectfully remind you,
Life and death are of supreme importance.
Time swiftly passes by and opportunity is lost.
Each of us should strive to awaken.
Awaken. Take heed. Do not squander your life.

— *Zen Mountain Monastery*[22]

We usually think of death as the physiological process whereby our heart stops beating, our lungs stop working, our brain function ceases, and we lose consciousness. This is the way I have always thought of it—in terms of the standard medical model. But after I was introduced to Zen, I learned of another kind of death. I heard that Zen training leads toward a diminishing of ego identity, with the prospect of eventual severance of ego attachment, a "spiritual death." What would that mean in my life?

While living and working in Nepal as a Peace Corps Volunteer, I kept up a routine of writing a letter to my parents once a week. I wrote each letter on a blue aerogramme, a combination of letter and envelope on which I would write my letter, crease it on the dotted lines, fold it up into an envelope, moisten the glued edges, and fasten it together. They were lightweight and already had airmail postage. I was having so many interesting exchanges with people in the village and so many adventures; it was always easy to write. I often had more to say than would fit onto the front and back sides of the aerogramme.

My parents saved all my letters and collected them in three-ring binders. Eventually they gave me the collection, and from time to time, decades later, I have reread the letters. The voice of this twenty-four-year-old young man sounds enthusiastic, wide-eyed, and energetic, as well as invincible, narcissistic, and arrogant. Today I am struck by the false quality of that identity. What seemed real then does not feel real any longer.

Over the years, when meeting new people, I often found myself telling stories of my experiences in Nepal. Using events in my past, I defined who I was, both to myself and to others. But as I repeated these stories again and again, they began to sound false—not that they were untrue, but that the repetition was tiresome; stories of my past felt less and less like the real "me."

Roshi says, "Without experiencing death, there is no true Zen practice." For me this means the gradual process of dropping identification with the stories I tell.

My zazen practice is counting my breath, bringing awareness to the pit of my belly, focusing on the bottom of each breath, letting my cognitive function quiet down and body awareness strengthen. I feel a growing capacity to let go of feelings of being hurt or resentful or proud. It's an ongoing process.

My practice is motivated by the possibility of realization of an ego death. And there is an extra boost of urgency springing from the contemplation of my physical death.

With regard to my own physical death, I anticipate being able to experience the changes that occur in my body and mind, including the progressive deterioration of my faculties up until, but probably not beyond, my final conscious moment. I doubt that I will experience anything after death. Of course, I cannot be positive about that, but my best guess is that awareness requires a live, functioning body. So I'm not counting on having any ongoing awareness at all after my physical death. The simplest assumption, which I embrace, is that dead means dead. If I'm wrong about that, I guess I'll find out eventually, but I am not counting on experiencing an afterlife. I am more concerned with trying to reap the benefits of Zen practice while I am still alive.

To me, the experience of a clear mind requires a living person. That seems obvious. But one day during a dharma talk, I was puzzled. Roshi seemed to allude to an all-encompassing mind that transcended death, and it didn't make any sense to me. So I put the question to him directly at sanzen. I said, "Roshi, I think that after I die I won't be able to experience any mind at all, let alone a clear mind." Without skipping a beat, he replied, "If that were true, then there would be no need to do zazen."

That stopped me in my tracks. To this day, I still haven't resolved the wisdom of his answer (if it is, in fact, wisdom). I thought to myself, "Well, if that's the way he thinks, then the two of us are miles apart." I even entertained the thought of giving up zazen altogether. But on further consideration, I knew that zazen practice was too important to turn my back on it due to conceptual dickering. So I put the exchange on the back shelf, labeled, "Things I will probably never understand."

This wasn't the only time that my worldview clashed with Roshi's. I remember one dharma talk where Roshi said, "Zen practice leads to supernatural powers." That statement really stuck in my craw. I knew that I needed to bring this up in sanzen because it was really bothering me.

The next time I saw Roshi, I said,

> "I need to know how best to make use of my point of view when listening or speaking. I definitely have my own point of view, based on my experiences. I presume you too have your own point of view. But when you make a statement like 'Zazen practice leads to supernatural powers,' I don't know where that is coming from. From my point of view,

supernatural powers do not exist. So it's impossible to develop them with zazen."

Roshi replied,

"This is important. We need to use extraneous thinking when we are explaining things to people. It's not as if this [supernatural power] is a real thing."

That helped me a bit. But later that day, right after our noon meal, I was handed a note by Chisan that cleared things up completely. I practically burst out laughing. It said,

Not to get too entangled on words, but, from a Zen poem: "Supernatural powers—drawing water, carrying wood."

Love, Chisan

That was exactly what I needed to hear. The issue disappeared, and everything suddenly felt crystal clear.

This experience made me realize that attachment to one's worldview is just one more thing we need to let go of.

In my meditation practice, I return again and again to the inner awareness of bodily sensations and mental thoughts, continually dropping the pursuit of endless dialogue and fantasies. I need to constantly bring my attention back to the breath, centering my consciousness low in the belly. Then gradually, over the course of days and weeks, my mind quiets down. Over time, the attachment to my stories, opinions, and worldviews gradually lessens. The conglomeration of images and psychological attributes that I habitually call my "self" becomes a bit unreal and arbitrary.

Roshi encourages his students to apply themselves diligently in this practice, aiming eventually to "die completely." He contends that only after having a direct experience of this can one awaken to a greater self, where one's identity has shifted from a narrow focus to a broad identity that encompasses all things.

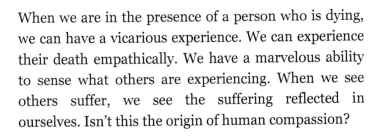

When we are in the presence of a person who is dying, we can have a vicarious experience. We can experience their death empathically. We have a marvelous ability to sense what others are experiencing. When we see others suffer, we see the suffering reflected in ourselves. Isn't this the origin of human compassion?

Addressing his students at Sogenji, Roshi said,

> "This experience of self-nature is experiencing
> no nature whatsoever. Everyone here at Sogenji
> is prepared with a solid base to realize this place
> where we are able to know from experience this
> true self—that it is an empty self. Not by
> discussing it or having preconceived notions
> about it, but to actually know that experience
> directly is what has to be the central point of all

of this. Everyone here has the potential to do that. People who don't yet have the faith, trust, and deep belief in this, please go to Tahoma and work at Enso House. By doing that you will see this right up front and have the deep faith and have the deep trust that is necessary."

Before Enso House came into being, Roshi had been encouraging his students to be involved with hospice care. Ed Lorah (Gentoku) had been working as a hospice care social worker and palliative care consultant. Ed says,

"For me, Zen practice and the practice of trying to be present with families when someone is dying are like two tree trunks wrapping around each other. I have no doubt that being a Zen student has made me a better hospice practitioner, and being a hospice practitioner has made me a better Zen student. The two things are inseparable.

"One of the important things for people in hospice work is presence—to really cultivate a sense of being empty when you go in to be with people in those kinds of situations. If you are quiet inside and just offer that to people, they respond.

"That's oftentimes the one thing they don't have in their family system: everything is on full boil. 'All of my family members have arrived from Miami, Grandma is dying.' People are really on edge. People in their fifties would say to me, 'I've never seen a dead body before.'

"What we do by being present with people is that we are actually normalizing things for them. People don't know what normality is when it comes to this, because normally your day-to-day life just runs unconsciously—you know, going to work, stopping at the store on the way home, making dinner, going to bed.

"For me, the ability to work with somebody like the Roshi is a gift. But it's not a free gift; it's not a gift that you use to go inside yourself and not come out. It's not about my enlightenment. It's about what I can translate into action for other people. When translating things into action, sometimes quietness is an action."

———◈◈◈———

In November 1999, Ed Lorah (Gentoku) came to Sogenji to sit a sesshin. As soon as he arrived, Chisan asked him to give a talk to the sangha about hospice care.

At the time, Taigan had been practicing at Sogenji for just over a year and had planned to extend for another year. He was there when Ed Lorah came to Sogenji to speak about hospice care.

Remembering Taigan, Chisan says,

"Taigan's life was transformed. I know the moment: in front of the kettles at Sogenji. Taigan's life was transformed by Gentoku. I remember him coming and saying, 'I want to do that.' Taigan really got turned on. Gentoku is very mild mannered, and rather understated, but for Taigan, who was a person of practice at that time, he found meaning in the idea that seeing death is an important part of training. Taigan felt that this was a process he wanted to participate in too."

Chisan encouraged Taigan to go to Whidbey Island and help start Enso House. A few years later, Taigan wrote a letter to Roshi describing his observations.

"Death, as I have come to see it, is actually very ordinary. It is just another moment in the infinite succession of moments that make up our lives. Death and dying become special and powerful not by virtue of the moment itself but by the amount of attention and energy that is given to these moments in our lives. Death seems to call and hold the attention of both the one who is dying and the family around the dying. This accumulation of attention and energy has an intense impact on those involved with the process: truths are seen easier, the past discords are often forgotten, and new relationships among family are born. But I believe that, like sesshin, one needs an environment that can give people the space and love to digest and take in the events and the accompanying energy. This is where I have seen both the value of a place like Enso House and found many parallels between it and Tahoma.

"Medically, nothing special is done here, certainly nothing different than what one may find in any hospice or nursing home in the nation. But the environment—one that provides people the time, attention, and space to process emotions, understand connections, and find peace—is, if not unique, very rare. Like Tahoma, this is the result of small things: a cup of tea here, a smile there, taking time to listen and really hear the person speaking. This may be a subjective observation, but I believe that friends, family, and residents, when faced with this attention, come to believe in the goodness of themselves and the goodness of the world around them. These intuitions may temporarily leave them when they return to the world, but I believe traces of their experience will always remain.

"Put simply, Enso House is a spiritual center. Enso provides a space that allows the resident and family to open themselves up, so that the energy, time, love, and emotions that are expressed during the dying process become fully available and integrated by everyone involved."

Taigan went on to enroll in nursing school and completed his RN. Subsequently he went on to work as a nurse at the Cedars-Sinai Medical Center in Los Angeles.

Later, another one of Roshi's students, Shojun (Teresa Hess), a young woman just out of college, was asked to be a caregiver at Enso House. She had some reluctance to leave Sogenji because she had not yet passed her first koan. She was concerned that leaving the monastery would get in the way of her spiritual training, but eventually agreed to go.

As it turned out, she had a rewarding experience as a caregiver. When asked if there was a connection between her Zen practice and her caregiving role, she said,

> "Oh, yes, completely—being in the moment, with people, not expecting, not knowing. Like I said, at Enso House we're supposed to be giving this spiritually conscious caregiving, and it's a challenge not to have a preset idea about what that means. To realize what that means is to be totally open to whatever the person wants or needs, to become one with them, to be able to intuit what they need even when they are in a place where they can't verbally communicate with you.
>
> "There is such a strong—I want to say— energetic thing that happens around the time of someone's passing where the room gets really full—when they are on the threshold. It's a similar feeling to a really good, strong zendo. We used to refer to it—what did we call it?— something like, the Death Vibe—and then everyone wants to be involved, all the

volunteers; it's such an amazing feeling. That's one of the things that dawned on me and blew me away working at Enso House: that death could be this really beautiful thing. I'd never seen anyone die before. It's a pretty taboo subject in our society. So, to see it first hand, and to see all the love that can come out of it, to see all the beauty that can happen as someone passes out of their body astounded me and really made a deep impression. It was life changing in that way."

I asked if Shojun thought the experience helped her with her first koan. She said,

"Yes! I think it did, actually. I passed my koan just a few weeks after I got back to Sogenji."

Hadrian Abbott was a Canadian student at Sogenji who volunteered to work as a caregiver at Enso House. Reflecting on his experience, he said,

"I learned a lot about human dignity, and the importance of each person being treated as a unique individual, and the importance of listening. There is no magic word that will make things better for the patient. Quite often, it is just listening.

"Before I came, the Roshi told me two things. The first was, when dealing with a resident, to see myself as the person in bed. I found that to be quite profound. I applied it at Enso House, and I try to apply it outside in general. I have found it has helped my practice enormously. It has broadened me.

"The second thing he told me was to see the things that I will never understand. And that's true; that applies to a lot of life. I stopped trying to understand things as soon as I got here. I just tried to do. I can reflect later. But it also helped to have the monastery next door, where I could go and sit every morning."

Chisan sees the practice of caregiving as fundamentally no different from the practice of doing pottery in the way she learned years ago in Japan. Becoming one with the tea bowl you are making is essentially the same practice as becoming one with the person you are caring for. She says,

"The practice of zazen allows you to learn on a cushion how to become completely one with your breath. When you are doing pottery in the Japanese style, you become the pot. You lose track of your body. You lose track of all your meditation. You throw the pot the same way you do your zazen, becoming your breath and your koan completely.

"In the practice of caregiving at Enso House, which is so intimately connected with the monastery, the key is in losing yourself completely. That may sound like a very facile thing to do: to lose yourself, to lose yourself in your pottery, to lose yourself in your caregiving. But it is not such an easy thing to understand, and it is not an easy thing to do. You learn how to do it. Each person needs to have a practice. One of the practices that is clearly aimed at being able to do that —lose yourself —is the practice of zazen."

MY FATHER'S FINAL DAYS

I agree with the preacher of Ecclesiastes that there is a time to love and a time to die—and when my skein runs out I hope to face the end calmly and in my own way. For most situations, however, I prefer the more martial view that death is the ultimate enemy—and I find nothing reproachable in those who rage mightily against the dying of the light.

—Stephen Jay Gould[23]

My father and mother lived in the same home for forty-six years. When they were in their late seventies, my sister Edie moved in and cared for them for the next ten years. However, as they approached their late eighties, it was clear the time had come for them to move into a facility for the elderly. The nearby Bonell Community run by the Good Samaritan Society looked like a good possibility. It had units for independent living, assisted living, skilled nursing, and hospice all on the same campus. They could share a one-bedroom apartment in the independent living area, and then as their needs grew, they could easily get additional care. Moving to a new place would also be an opportunity to adjust some non-optimal living habits.

It had always been important for Dad to be in charge of family finances. He kept his checkbook in his left shirt pocket at all times. In many ways he was miserly, in others quite generous, but most important to him was having control. Even though Mom and Dad were well off, he worried that without his oversight, their fortune would soon disappear. Unfortunately, he balked at spending money on home maintenance projects such as hiring an inspector to look into termite dust in the basement, replacing an aging inefficient furnace, and putting on a new roof.

Instead of having his fully capable daughter, Edie, make spending decisions, he gave her (and Mom) a monthly allowance. Dad was losing his ability to monitor the bills, and Edie had been taking on greater responsibility for finances over the years. The situation was becoming untenable. So through some deft compassionate coaxing and negotiation, Edie arranged their life transition to Bonell. Moving there made it possible for Dad to let go of his role of overseeing the money.

At Bonell there was no Wi-Fi available, and I thought that this might help Dad simplify his life since he had been spending many frustrating hours going through his email inbox and deleting spam. He also used his computer, however, for mind stimulating activities such as writing and taking notes from *Scientific American* articles. So, within three days after moving, Dad was asking about having a DSL line installed and getting his computer and printer set up once again.

When he moved into Bonell, Dad was having a bit of difficulty with walking and balance, and started using a cane. His heart was growing weaker. He felt out of breath even after moderate exercise. But his most serious disability (and greatest embarrassment) was incontinence. With loss of bladder control came the need to wear absorbent briefs and to deal with changing them every few hours.

At first, Dad tried to limit his use of disposable diapers by lining them with cloth towels, but that strategy resulted in an upsurge of daily laundry. Mom was taking on more and more responsibility for doing the laundry and keeping him dry. She began to feel exhausted with her role as caregiver—fixing his breakfast and supper, helping him dress, shower, and use the toilet. Also, Dad's sleep-wake cycle was getting out of sync with hers; he wanted to work late into the night on his writing projects; she wanted to get a full eight hours of sleep. It was becoming increasingly difficult to live with him.

One day, Dad got up in the middle of the night to use the bathroom but left his cane behind. While returning to bed, he fell down hard on the floor and fractured his femur. In the hospital, doctors performed surgery to reinforce the bone. Dad was instructed not to put weight on his leg for six weeks and he was moved to the STAR Care facility[24] at Bonell Community for rehabilitation. During rehab, the STAR Care staff did their best to attend to his incontinence while providing physical therapy, but still there were times when he sat in a wet diaper for hours.

One night, a nurse found Dad slumped over on his bed, and concerned that he had had a stroke, she called an ambulance to take him to the emergency room. After doing an electrocardiogram and some blood tests, doctors discovered that he had suffered a heart attack sometime within the past twenty-four hours. They also found that he had a bladder infection, which may have put some extra strain on his heart. The heart attack had been completely painless. The infection was an antibiotic-resistant MRSA strain of bacteria that required intravenous vancomycin (the "drug of last resort") to treat, an infection he must have been exposed to in the hospital or rehab facility. After treatment at the hospital, Dad felt better and couldn't seem to understand what all the fuss was about and why he was "locked up in just one little room."

Dad was extremely weak, and he tired quickly. With a weakened heart, operating at only about 40 percent of capacity, he was experiencing congestive heart failure. On Saturday, after returning from the hospital, a nurse coaxed him to walk to the bathroom using his walker. She had to steady him while he walked the few steps and when he returned to his bed, he was exhausted. The next morning, he seemed to have perked up. He was cheerfully eating his breakfast of eggs and pancakes, coffee and apple juice when Edie came to see him.

I arrived from Seattle and saw Dad in the hospital. Dad's hair had turned snowy white; I didn't see any of the dark hair he still had up until a few years ago. His eyes were sunken in their sockets, red around the edges. He was eating small portions of food and his weight was gradually dropping. Soon after I arrived, he transitioned to eating only soft foods and he had to be monitored closely during meals. He stopped making the trip to the dining room and since a caregiver was unavailable to assist during mealtimes, a family member needed to be present.

Usually, if I encouraged him to eat and touched his lips with a spoon, he would open his mouth and take in the food. I could sometimes get five to six spoonfuls into his mouth before he would fall asleep or tell me that was enough. I sometimes wondered to myself, "What is the point of pressuring him to eat if he has no interest in it?" Obviously, his body functions were slowing, and his systems of eating, chewing, swallowing, and digesting were shutting down.

I realized my behavior was interconnected with his. His lack of interest in eating reduced my level of interest in feeding him. However, if I stopped feeding him, he didn't indicate a desire for any more food. The more I pushed him to eat, the more he ingested, but I began questioning my motivation for encouraging him to eat. Would more food overload his digestive system with foods it could no longer break down? Would pushing food on him extend his dying process for a few more days? I continued to feed him because the two of us were entangled in a dance of sorts. Sometimes I wondered whether I even had any free will at all in this matter.

A week later, a number of family members arrived to see Dad. He was able to meet his eight-month-old great-granddaughter, Anna and his spirits lifted. We whipped up an impromptu party in the care facility where we ordered takeout Italian food. We were able to all visit together and Dad seemed glad to have an audience for a few of his stories.

About two thirty the next morning, Edie received a call from a nursing assistant who had found Dad having difficulty breathing and called an ambulance. When we arrived at the hospital, the physician explained that his breathing had been reduced by an accumulation of fluid in his lungs, likely brought on by having too much salt in the body. After receiving an intravenous diuretic drug, Dad felt better and seemed puzzled as to why there had been so much commotion and why he had been sent to the emergency room. Apparently, incidents of breathing difficulty due to fluid retention are quite common and easily treatable. We just had no idea of the risk we were taking by sharing Italian takeout food.

Although Dad had received excellent care in the hospital, the experience was traumatic— the ambulance ride, an IV line inserted in his arm, a Foley catheter inserted into his urethra, being confined to bed, being constantly awakened to have his vital signs checked. Back in STAR care, he suffered from considerable confusion as to where he was and where his family was. We were determined to spare Dad any more trips to the ER.

As a result of Dad's episodes with health crises, Edie and I decided it was time to learn more about Dad's local opportunities for hospice. There was a hospice associated with the rehab facility that was caring for 650 patients annually, serving three Colorado counties. The whole family met with a hospice nurse in Dad's room who described the services they provided and talked about the process of determining hospice eligibility. We learned that a patient was eligible for hospice when their heart was functioning at 30 percent capacity or less. At the most recent measurement, Dad's was at 40 percent. When she asked if anyone had any questions, Dad raised his hand and said, "I didn't understand a thing that was said." It was probably a combination of being hard of hearing, having difficulty following rapid speech, and making logical sense of what was being said. It was sad to see Dad so helpless and a stark reminder of how vulnerable we become in our final years.

Dad was in good hands at the rehab unit, and it was time for me to return to Seattle. A couple of weeks later, we had a conference call with STAR Care staff about Dad's care. The speech therapist explained that she was working with Dad to help develop his skills of conversing—paying attention when someone else is speaking, waiting until they were finished before interrupting, and speaking appropriately. Dad made a career of teaching, speaking, and writing. Now, it was as if he were a young child needing special remedial help.

The speech therapist also mentioned that Dad was focused on his book. He had persuaded his nurses to let him use his computer so that he could do his writing but he would get frustrated and constantly needed assistance. Edie and I and my Mom were all too familiar with this pattern. Dad had difficulty remembering the steps even for the simplest tasks on his computer. He was frustrated because he knew he had been capable of all these things in the past, but now they exceeded his capacity. The nurses explained that sometimes Dad worked late into the night with his computer, and that this late night activity interfered with his sleep and made him cranky during the day.

The occupational therapist had the same take on the situation. She thought it would be best if the computer were removed from his room, so it would not be such a distraction. Edie and I agreed with them—it would be better to remove the computer.

While Dad listened to all this at the conference, he didn't speak up. He just stared at the floor with a look of annoyance on his face. Later, he called our daughter,

Sarah and complained that the nurse and therapists didn't understand the importance of his book writing. He said, "What they don't understand is that I am Les Trowbridge. I am Les Trowbridge!"

Over the next few weeks, Dad's condition continued to deteriorate. His doctor determined that he qualified for hospice; his heart was functioning at less than 30 percent capacity. Cynthia and I returned to Colorado. We imagined that this might be the last time we would see him.

Dad is lying on his right side, facing the wall in room 227 of the STAR Care facility. I greet him as I sit on the side of the bed and put my hand on his shoulder, "Hi, Dad!"

"Who is it?" he asks, aroused from a stupor, trying to get his orientation of place and time.

"It's David. Cynthia and I came down here to see you."

"You came down to see me? That's wonderful."

There is a palpable sense of relief in the room following this exchange of greetings, as it confirms that we can still recognize each other and connect. Having my hand on his shoulder is slightly more intimate than our usual rather limited physical contact. Generally, Dad's habit is to extend his hand for a handshake with his sons.

I notice some white powder around his lips, which seem very dry. "Would you like a sip of water?" I ask. He is eager for a drink of water, which he sips through a soda straw. Generally, Dad wants to keep his sippy cup close so that he is not dependent on anyone else.

My immediate impression is that Dad has grown substantially weaker since I saw him four weeks ago. Now he prefers to just lie in bed, always on his right side with a pillow tucked up under his right cheek. His rehabilitation program has been discontinued. His condition has declined in spite of the conscientious efforts by rehab specialists to bring him back to the level of functioning he had before his hip fracture and before his heart attack.

"Could I have some more water?" he asks. "Of course, Dad. Here you go." I lift the cup and bring the soda straw to his lips. He takes several sips.

I move my hands in small circles on his shoulder. He doesn't object. Slowly, I start to rub his back. "How does that feel, Dad?" "It feels good," he says. I realize that this is the first time I have ever given my father a back rub. He is ninety-one years old. As long as I can remember, I have never had this much intimate physical contact with my father. He is making soft moaning sounds, almost like singing. He clearly likes the back rub, which I am happy to continue. Cynthia and I have a long habit of giving each other back rubs, and I am grateful to her for cultivating this part of my being. Now I have a chance to share this simple pleasure with my Dad.

Dad says consistently that he has no pain. Even when the nurses turn him over, and he winces and moans, he still insists that he feels no pain. He has started to develop bed sores from lying in his preferred position. There are three sores on his right foot: on the ankle bone, the top of the foot, and the side of the foot near the toes.

As I gently rub his back today, he says, "Keep doing that." We sit together a long time as I alternate massaging the muscles of his upper back on either side of his spine and giving him sips of water. Finally he asks, "What do I do now?"

I explain that breakfast will be arriving soon and that he might be having some applesauce or ice cream. But then I think, this may be an opportunity to widen the subject a bit. Maybe he needs to be reminded that his family is fine—that it's okay to let go of his concerns. So I try to assure him: his wife has a nice place to live and is happy there; Edie is content in a comfortable home. Everyone has been taken care of, and it is fine to let go now. I'm not sure whether my words or meaning get through. He doesn't show any overt signs that he understands, and he doesn't give any verbal response, but I'm glad I have started the discussion about letting go.

The certified nursing assistants (CNAs) have put padded booties on his feet to try to reduce the pressure on his bedsores. But they are bulky and hot. Dad finds them uncomfortable. When I ask him if he wants me to remove them, he asks, "What is the objective?" He wants to understand the reasoning behind wearing the booties. If there is a good reason, then, of course, he is willing to wear them. But he is skeptical, and if the rationale is weak, he would like them removed immediately. Just like Dad.

A nursing assistant named Jill comes in to check his belly and reports that it seems distended, perhaps due to gas or constipation. She tells Dad she has come in to take a look at his tummy. Dad says, "You want to look at my beautiful tummy?" We have a hearty laugh. I am reminded of how similar his sense of humor is to my own.

Dad's eyes open wide; he looks directly at me and extends his arm. I clasp his hand. He says, "I want to tell you I appreciate your being here."

"It's my pleasure, Dad," I tell him.

He then asks me, "How did you get latched onto this?"

It's an interesting question; Dad has an image of his son as a teacher, a scientist, an explorer, an adventurer, but not a caregiver. The tone of his question suggests that taking care of a dying person is not something I would have chosen to do, but something I got roped into doing.

I tell him that it may have started with my experience in Nepal on the mountain climbing expedition when I nearly died in a rock fall. It made me realize how fragile life is and how impermanent. He smiles knowingly.

This morning, when I put the soda straw in his mouth to offer him water, he seems to forget how to suck a straw. I tell him, "Close your lips. Suck." At first, it doesn't register. Then he closes his lips and recalls how to draw up liquid through the straw.

After about three days of not eating, I conclude that he will eat no more. I have lost track of how many meals have been discarded after he has turned them down. Then one afternoon, a nursing assistant shows up with a Magic Cup, a nutrient concoction with the consistency of ice cream, and suggests that Leslie might like to have some. I start to tell her that Dad has stopped eating, but then I hold my tongue. She puts one spoonful after another to his lips; he opens his mouth and eats it without any problem. Just when I thought I had it all figured out, he surprises us once again. Thoughts tumble through my head: "Here you have been starving the old man!"

<hr />

One afternoon as I sit with Dad, he opens his eyes, but they are not seeing eyes—they strike me as the eyes of a dead person. I stroke the top of his head and hold his hand. His heart is still beating, and his lungs are still working. I can see a pulse under the skin on his neck, and his shoulders rise and fall with each breath. I match my own breathing with the rhythm of his. I start humming a tune that comes from I don't know where. It turns into a church hymn; I start singing with the same energy I used to use in the congregation of the First United Methodist Church in Greeley, Colorado. I'm singing a hymn but I don't know its name or whether I have ever heard it before, let alone sung it before. But it sounds like a hymn just the same. I'm sure Dad hears it, though he doesn't show any outward sign. He neither approves nor disapproves of it. I try to think of songs he might like to hear. I sing him the children's song familiar to children in many Christian Churches:

Jesus loves me! This I know,

For the Bible tells me so.

Little ones to him belong;

They are weak, but he is strong.

Yes, Jesus loves me!

Yes, Jesus loves me!

Yes, Jesus loves me!

The Bible tells me so.

It must have been nearly sixty years ago that I learned that song in Sunday school. I probably haven't got the words right, but it doesn't matter. There is a faint smile on Dad's lips. Tears are flowing down my cheeks, and I choke up on some of the words of the song. Dad just looks at me.

The words continue to reverberate in my mind after I stop singing. Are they reverberating through Dad's mind as well? I hope so, because I'll be leaving him now; it's about time for me to meet Mom and drive over to Edie's place for some soup for dinner.

Will Dad still be alive when I return this evening?

Dad is still breathing. No one has brought in any food for him or tried to feed him. I ask him if he would like to eat some applesauce. He says, "That would be fine." I open an applesauce cup and put a spoon to his mouth. He opens his mouth, and I spoon it in. But he doesn't chew. The applesauce just sits in his mouth. I put a cup of water with a soda straw to his lips, but he doesn't pucker his lips or suck on the straw. This may have been his last bite. Using a syringe, I slowly squeeze a couple of milliliters of water into his mouth. He swallows. Thank goodness, he can still swallow water.

I will be spending the night in Dad's room. I've brought in a foam mattress, a sleeping bag, and a meditation cushion. Dad is feeling sleepy, so I turn out the lights, leaving only a dim nightlight still glowing. After Dad falls asleep, I begin sitting in meditation. After about an hour, a nursing assistant arrives to check on Dad. She snaps on the lights and calls his name. "Leslie! Here to check your vitals!" she announces.

The instant she notices me sitting cross-legged on the floor, she jumps back with a start. I refrain from saying, "Oh, that's all right." Then after sizing up the situation, she goes about her business of changing Dad's briefs, turning him over, and repositioning the oxygen tubes in his nose. It's disturbing for Dad to have to be awakened so abruptly.

Word of the cross-legged relative in room 227 spreads among the staff. Gradually they learn to check his vital signs in the dim light and speak in soft voices.

Between interruptions from the staff, I try to get some sleep. But just before I do, I hear Dad calling, "Water, water." I know I need to get up and help him take a sip. This happens repeatedly and each time, his oxygen tubes have been pulled out and need to be replaced. After seeing to his needs, I turn out the lights and crawl back into my sleeping bag on the air mattress beside the bed. Within about five minutes, he is calling out, "Water! I need water!" So I get up, check the clock (about three o'clock) and see that he has pulled out the oxygen tubes again. I offer him some water, but he barely takes any at all. I resecure the oxygen tubes and go back to bed, hoping that now at last I can get some sleep.

Just then, the oxygen generator stops running. A red light comes on, and a loud beeping alarm goes off. I check the oxygen hoses, which seem okay, but the alarm keeps blasting. I go out to find a nurse and find Debbie, who comes in to check on the oxygen generator. She puts the outlet ports to her lips to try to sense the oxygen flow but feels nothing. She says she will go down and find a replacement unit. We turn off the power to the failed unit, and the incessant beeping finally stops. I wrap up the cord. She leaves to fetch a replacement.

It turns out the replacement units are not where she expects them to be, so she takes longer than expected. I feel like I may pass out on my feet. About twenty minutes later, she returns with another unit. We plug it in, turn it on, and connect the oxygen lines to Dad's nostrils.

I ask Debbie when the last time was that Dad had his medication (Roxanol, or morphine sulfate). I realize that my primary motivation is to get Dad to stop asking for water and stop pulling out the oxygen tubes from his nose so that I have a chance to get some sleep.

I share the dilemma that people caring for the dying must feel all over the world: when you are exhausted and sleep deprived, when your patient is agitated and inconsolable, and you have medication that will quiet the patient, you ask yourself: who am I doing this for?

Cynthia takes a turn spending the night in Dad's room. He has been restless for the past sixteen hours or so—asking for water, pulling his sheets and blanket off, pulling off his oxygen tubes. Several times, Dad says, "I want to go home." I come over at around seven o'clock in the morning to check on the two of them.

Dad says, "I don't know what to do. Where am I? What is going on?"

Cynthia says, "All you need to do now is to let go. Now you are free to join your mom and your brothers."

"I don't know what's happening."

I decide to be a little more direct and avoid the euphemism.

"Dad," I say, "You have come to the end of your life. Now you are dying."

"I'm dying? Really?" he asks.

"Yes, you are dying."

"Are you kidding?" he says. For a moment, it seems like this is the first time this fact has entered his consciousness.

"We all die, Dad. Your mom and your brothers, Charles and Bob, have died. Now you are dying. We all die."

He ponders this. He is not frightened or panicky. He is just taking in this information, apparently with equanimity. It's just another interesting thought to him. He actually seems less anxious now, less upset than he was before this very frank exchange.

<hr />

As soon as the nursing assistant finishes securing Dad's oxygen tubes, she leaves and he pulls them out again.

He says to me, "We have to talk."

"What do you want to talk about, Dad?"

"Why do I have to do this?" he asks.

"We all have to die when it's our turn," I say. "Your mom died when it was her turn; your brothers died. When it's my turn, I will die. Now it's your turn."

"I'm not ready," he says. "I have a book to write."

I tell him, "I'm writing the book, Dad. I'm telling our stories in the book."

"You're ninety-two years old, Dad. Your parents gave you birth; you gave us birth; we gave birth to our children. It's all part of evolution. We're all part of the big system." I ask him, "You know where your body came from, right Dad? The atoms in your body, the oxygen, carbon, nitrogen—all came from supernovae. You taught me this. Now it's time for those atoms to go back to making other bodies."

Cynthia calls me in the middle of the night while caring for Dad and tells me to come in. Dad's breathing has changed. There are lengthy pauses when he stops breathing. He takes a few deep breaths, and then his breath ceases again.

Edie and I arrive. We alternate sitting in the chair next to Dad's bed, holding his hand, rubbing his back, and stroking his head.

As the sun rises, Cynthia opens the drapes and sees a clear blue sky. "It's a beautiful day!"

As I hold his hand, Dad says, "Tell me how to do this."

I say, "Just relax into it. Everything is fine. It's a beautiful clear day, and everything is perfect. Everything has been taken care of. There is nothing else to do."

Edie says, "Just as the yogis do, you can simply drop your body."

Dad asks, "Do I have to say anything?"

Cynthia, "You want to do it right, don't you? And you are."

I say, "You can find out for yourself. You can experience it, Dad."

Shortly after eight o'clock, my mother comes up to see Dad.

Mom says, "Hello, Leslie. It's your Sweetie. Are you ready to say your good-byes?"

Dad replies, "Good-byes?"

He grasps her arm tightly with his clenched hand, then grabs the same arm with his other hand. He is holding on very tightly, borderline painfully. Mom takes it in stride.

Mom says, "We have had a wonderful life together. We have wonderful children. I will look after your published works."

Dad says, "That's wonderful."

Mom says, "Now it's time to close this chapter and say good-bye."

It appears to me that Dad is holding on for dear life. He really is fighting.

At a quarter past ten, a nursing assistant arrives and offers to serve Dad some Magic Cup. He says, "Okay," and then proceeds to eat about a third of a cup of this ice cream-like confection. I can hardly believe it. Just when I thought he was within hours of death, he displays a hearty appetite! This all seems interminable.

I'm sleeping on an inflatable mattress in Dad's room. At around three o'clock in the morning, I suddenly hear him ask, rather clearly and forcefully, "What was that all about yesterday?" He still hasn't accepted the inevitability of his death.

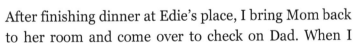

Cynthia and I need to decide whether to cancel our flight to Seattle or not. Our return reservation is for tomorrow, but it looks like Dad is going to be around for a while longer. I ask Dad, "How long do you want to live? Another month? Another week? Another day?"

Dad says, very clearly, "I want to live another month."

Cynthia and I decide to take Dad at his word. We plan to return home.

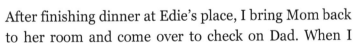

After finishing dinner at Edie's place, I bring Mom back to her room and come over to check on Dad. When I enter his room, out of the corner of my eye, I see that his bed is empty! What the...? Then I see him sprawled out on the floor, his head resting on the metal bar of the rolling service table. He has a stunned look on his face. I rush out the door and wave my arms to call a nursing assistant to come help me.

When the nursing assistant sees Dad on the floor, he's shocked. He tells me that he isn't allowed to touch a patient in this condition until the patient has been checked by a nurse. He summons Stacy, the RN on duty, and another nursing assistant, a young woman who has assisted Dad before.

Stacy checks Dad's body. She doesn't find any broken bones. A Hoyer lift is brought into the room, and the three staff members place the sling under Dad's body. They slip the green and blue straps over the hooks and position Dad in the middle of the sling. The hydraulic mechanism raises Dad's body up over the bed. I put my hand on his arm and notice how stiff it feels, almost as if he has lost the mobility of his arms.

Dad lies in bed with his mouth open and his eyes rolled back, his eyelids closed halfway. He is still breathing. The hospice nurse who stops by at around one in the morning thinks he will probably die before dawn. She says the mottled appearance of his skin is an indication that he has only hours more to live.

I have to consider again whether we should catch our flight to Seattle. On the one hand, I really would like to be here with Dad when he takes his last breath. It seems like I get only one chance and that it's important for me to witness this, if at all possible. On the other hand, I probably have an attachment to the idea. There is an equally good opportunity here for me to let go of that idea. Will I harbor regrets for leaving Dad before he has passed away?

Is there something special in witnessing another person's final breath? How will I feel later if I decide to leave my frustrating and irritable father behind to die by himself? If I am around during his final moments, I will be able to say something about what I observe; if not, then I won't be able to say anything. Is this important? Who is to say?

I gather my things and start packing up. Dad is no longer communicative, and it's probably just a matter of hours before he passes away. It's time to go.

I feel I have already grieved. Perhaps I will have feelings of grief again in the coming days. But right now, everything seems okay. Dad is breathing his last, and I am grateful that he will finally get some relief from his suffering. Is "relief" the right word? Certainly being dead means that you will not experience suffering. But that really isn't the same as experiencing relief. I believe he won't experience that either. But from the perspective of those of us still living, we can see a completion to one man's life—a natural phase after a long and event-filled life. It doesn't seem tragic, and it is certainly not unexpected. For the circle of friends and family members who have been caring for him, his death brings palpable relief. His decline in health has meant an increasing burden on many people, and soon that will all end. Why would any one of us wish for his life to continue any longer?

I feel grateful to have had the opportunity to be this close to Dad's death. I relish the direct perception of this aspect of reality and cherish my experience. It hasn't been clouded by intense emotion, and I value that—I believe my experience is closer to the truth when it is dispassionate. That probably says a lot about who I am.

Cynthia and I catch the 12:25 Alaska Airlines flight back to Seattle. Dad would understand. He always put getting things done as the highest priority, and he shunned sentimentality. He definitely would want us to carry on with our lives, which is what I have chosen to do. Cynthia would have been fine either way; she has unlimited patience being with people who need assistance. But she has left the decision of whether to stay or go up to me.

As I am wont to do, I also think about what Roshi would do. It seems pretty clear that after doing what was appropriate under the circumstances, he would carry on with his commitments. I feel that this is what I am doing. So I am relieved to be returning to my life on

Whidbey Island. But at the same time, I feel a twinge of regret that I am leaving my father to die alone.

Returning to my daily schedule in Seattle, I am amazed at how quickly my attention shifts from concerns about Dad to the usual demands of daily life. The first couple of days back, I really don't think much about Dad at all.

Two days later, Edie calls to let me know that the situation is still pretty much the same. She and Mom have visited Dad both days. He is uncommunicative but shows some response when she announces her presence. He is not eating or drinking anything.

The next day, February 3, Edie calls and says, "That's the end. Dad passed away this morning. At nine o'clock, a nursing assistant came in and saw that he was breathing very rapidly, so they gave him a dose of his medication. When they came in at nine thirty, he had passed."

So he did indeed pass away alone—on his mother's birthday.

In Greenbank on Whidbey Island, the sky is clearing. A clear sky always starts me thinking about opening up the observatory. After dark, the moon will be in a good place for observing. Jupiter will be high in the sky,

Venus very bright in the west, also remarkably high. It would be a good time to invite people to come up and look through the telescope. Unfortunately, I feel drained of energy and not particularly excited about spending an evening at the telescope. Then I think about how important Dad has been for cultivating my interest in astronomy and teaching. Wouldn't a star party be the best way to honor Dad's memory? I decide to call up some people and invite them over.

I start up my planetarium program and search for my latest copy of *Sky and Telescope* magazine to check on the configuration of Jupiter's moons. Europa and Io are presently to the east of the planet; Ganymede and Callisto, to the west. Io is extremely close to the limb of Jupiter and moving slowly closer. In fact at 9:01 p.m. Pacific Time, Io will begin passing across the face of the planet—an ideal time to be watching. Just past first quarter phase, the moon is gibbous and fairly high in the sky—excellent for viewing. Venus shines bright above the western horizon.

Dairin, at the monastery, says he can bring over others after they finish evening zazen. Our friends Gary and Rubye, and Miriam and John, and our neighbor, Deborah, can come. So it should be a good group.

The sky is clear in the early evening, and the guests who arrive early get an excellent view of the moon and planets. Then some high clouds start to appear, so the later guests, including our friends from the monastery, see images diminished in clarity through clouds. Nevertheless they can see the moons of Jupiter, the dark bands across the face of the planet, and Io kissing the limb. The craters of the moons can be seen relatively well, in spite of the fact that we are looking through clouds. Then we retire inside to warm up and have some dessert.

Cynthia serves vanilla ice cream with Bailey's Irish Cream, as she remembers my Dad used to love that dessert combination. We pass around a photograph of my parents' wedding—my Dad looks so young. He was only twenty-six when they married. I tell some stories of growing up, especially my memories of doing science projects with my Dad. It's a fitting close to this remembrance. Then it's time for the guys to return to the monastery—they will need to be up by five o'clock. Our guests say their good-byes. As the last car drives away, I look up at the great sky above and see that the clouds have once again disappeared, and the moon, the planets, and the stars all shine brightly once again.

Epilogue: Lessons Learned

Learn to die and you shall live,
for there shall be none
who learn to truly live
who have not learned to die.

—*The Book of the Craft of Dying*[25]

B ack in 2001 when we bought the property that would become Enso House, there wasn't any assurance this undertaking would pan out. All we had to go on was faith that things would develop in a positive way. We trusted Roshi's vision of a place for hospice care and imagined that he would soon be leaving Sogenji, moving to Whidbey Island and bringing with him Zen students who would be available as caregivers.

I remember having some rather grandiose ideas of how large the project would become. I envisioned a paid staff, with five or six patients in residence—six was the maximum allowed by our Adult Family Home license. I expected that most patients would be with us for a few months, after having a prognosis of less than six months to live, and that once we developed a successful business model, other groups around the country and the world would want to replicate it.

Now I think we can lay claim to having probably the worst business model in the world. Not to say that things don't work—they work remarkably well. It's just that we realize we are not a business.

During the formative years of Enso House, our volunteer finance expert, George Moseley, worked with Ann to prepare spreadsheets with projected revenues and expenses. In order to develop a plausible model for how this was going to work, they tried to anticipate how many paying guests we would have at any one time, how many paid staff, what their hourly pay rates would be, and so forth. This required coming up with a work schedule of rotating shifts that gave caregivers sufficient time off to recover between shifts.

We contemplated hiring someone who would be responsible for "development" and to organize fundraising events throughout the year—someone who could bring in the sums of money we expected to need for operations.

One by one our assumptions collapsed. From its earliest days, people have chosen to work at Enso house for personal satisfaction, not to earn a living. Our various scenarios involving paid staff seemed to be irrelevant in light of the commitments made by our volunteers.

Enso House has always attracted people who want to volunteer. Many, I think, have been inspired by our physician, Ann Cutcher, and her decision to volunteer full-time to the project. Our nurse, MyoO, has made the same commitment and has also volunteered full-time.

And, thanks to the vigorous recruitment efforts of Chisan, we have almost always had a third core caregiver available, selected from among Roshi's students at Sogenji. However, the scenario I imagined of Roshi moving to Whidbey Island and taking up residence at Tahoma Monastery has not come to pass. I have finally let go of that expectation and have come to accept that Enso House will be a small project for the foreseeable future, taking care of one patient at a time.

Now that Dairin has officially been installed as Assistant Abbot of Tahoma-san Sogenji Zen Monastery, there is greater stability and greater opportunity for integrating caregiving at Enso House with Zen training at the monastery. Over time, we hope to see more people from the Seattle area serving as volunteer caregivers.

In the first couple of years after we opened our doors, there were occasions when we had two guests at once, but those were the exception. Hosting two guests was stressful on our core caregiving staff. When both required intensive twenty-four-hour care, it was untenable. Increasingly, Ann accepts guests only on a one-at-a-time basis. It became more common to have periods of time when we had no guests at all for weeks at a time. This has continued to be the pattern of caregiving at Enso House. It has meant that the core caregivers have had time to recharge and summon the energy needed for the next guest.

One guest in residence at a time has meant that each receives undivided twenty-four-hour care, and family members can spend as much time as they want with their loved one without having to worry about meals or accommodations. Because we have an available physician and nurse in the house at all times, medications are monitored and dosages are adjusted as needed on a continual basis.

So what can we say specifically about lessons we learned? The first lesson we have learned is that staying small is essential for delivering the kind of care we do. We realize that our situation came about through serendipity and cannot necessarily be replicated. A physician and nurse who have devoted themselves to serving at Enso House and a Zen roshi who has committed to providing Zen students to serve as caregivers as part of their training are unique gifts.

The second lesson is that our responsibilities go beyond caring for patients during their final days. It is equally important to care for family members and friends who are going through difficult times: coping with exhaustion, vulnerability and grief. Simply providing a quiet environment and hot meals can work wonders. A confident caregiving team and kind volunteers convey a sense that things will be okay. By turning over the caregiving responsibilities to Enso House, family members can be more present with their loved one and are able to return to their familiar role prior to the onset of the illness. This is a huge benefit.

The third lesson has to do with the place of Enso House in the local community. Neighbors have responded generously to requests for help with remodeling and construction projects, fundraising events, newsletter mailings, and the day-to-day chores of cooking, cleaning, recycling, garbage collection, and landscaping. Without consciously trying to do so, Enso House has become a kind of community center on South Whidbey. At times when there is no guest in residence, people are free to come and go as they please, just to have a cup of tea and chat. People feel comfortable coming to Ann Cutcher for guidance about all kinds of age-related health issues. Her efforts to attend funerals and memorial services for guests have helped maintain a consistent presence in the community.

Finally, we have learned the wisdom of not being attached to our ideas of what constitutes a "good death," our expectations about how dying progresses, or our plans for the future. Each guest who comes to Enso House reminds us once again about how mysterious and unknowable the sacred process of life and death really is.

AFTERWORD BY SHODO HARADA ROSHI

I die every day.

—St. Paul[26]

Neither Enso House nor this book would have come to fruition were it not for the vision of Shodo Harada Roshi. I asked him to speak to this project. He begins with the words of his teacher, Mumon Yamada:

"Feeling that the day was somehow unusually pleasant, I moved to the porch to enjoy the fresh air, the wafting breeze that came across the porch, blowing through the white heavenly bamboo flowers. What a great feeling breeze! An indescribably wonderful feeling came to me, and a thought arose. In this weak, sickness-stricken body, I was struck by the question, 'What is this wonderful breeze?'

"And then a thought occurred to me—I was so deeply struck, it was as if I had been hit with an iron bar! 'This breeze! It is air!' While this body was so ridden with sickness, I could barely sit up straight. I became riveted to the thought, 'This breeze is air; there is always air!' Everyone had abandoned me, but there was still air, which never has left me alone, not even for a single second. And it's not just me; everyone is held like this. We cannot live only by our own bodies; we are all embraced and given life by a huge power.

"Usually when we think of air, it is only an idea about air. This most precious air, without which we cannot live for even one minute—it is so important and yet we take it for granted! All day and all night without any break whatsoever, whether we are working or resting or sleeping or waking, we may forget it, but air has never ever forgotten us!"

Realizing this so deeply and totally and seeing how true it was, he wanted to shout it to the skies. A new energy and motivation rose up in him. Without even thinking about it, the words came out of his mouth,

Oh Great All Embracing Mind!

A clear realization,

Brought to me by this morning's cool wafting breeze.

This is the writing of my teacher, Mumon Yamada Roshi, when he told about his own experience. My teacher almost died from tuberculosis. He was on death's edge for a long time; for years he lived with this threat. Then in this life of sickness, he discovered a deep truth that he expressed with these words.

People are born, and then they live their whole lives facing death. How many people are truly full of joy? Most people are melancholy and face the end of their life thinking that it is the end of everything. But life is not something melancholy. We each have received and are always receiving grace from so many others in order to stay alive—it is immeasurable.

At Enso House, grace is delivered by those people who help take care of guests nearing the end of life. A professional doctor and nurse are on duty twenty-four hours a day. What is important there is that the caregivers and those who are dying are connected by prayer.

Zazen is prayer, and while it is sometimes done by crossing the legs, zazen is not our body sitting—it is our mind sitting. We are letting everything go except today's life, being it completely and not looking away from it—not speaking, not doing, but seeing that with which we are born, our pure true nature—this is zazen.

The Sixth Patriarch defined zazen. He said that it is to not give added ideas of anything, such as good or bad, to things which we perceive, and to not hold any concerns about anything at all in our inner mind.

For beginners, we teach it as one breath and then the next breath, cultivating one's abdominal breathing. Our breath comes and goes, our breathing fills us with full ki energy, and we have this full tautness so whatever problems we may encounter externally or internally, we are not moved around. Everything appears like a reflection in a mirror—the same as in our death, it is not about the form of our body. All day long we do zazen.

The Sixth Patriarch says that in zazen we reflect the external world; we do not bring in anything extraneous or hold on to any idea of a "me"; otherwise we will be moved around by that. When we get angry, we get red; when we get afraid, we get blue; our pulse gets faster; our body is pulled around by concepts. But if we are full and taut doing zazen, then when we work, we only work. Then there is no more separation and no more confusion. We are not self-referring, but rather, we are like a mirror that only reflects and remains empty-minded.

In the Yuikyo-gyo (Legacy Teachings Sutra) the Buddha wrote,

> For all of us, to be born into this world is to encounter death. Don't be sad. Even if we have one whole kalpa to live in this life, it is the same thing. Everyone we ever meet, we will have to part with; without fail we will separate.

The Buddha at the age of twenty-nine felt that humanity's pain and suffering could not be left as it is, that there must be some reason for humans' conflicts, some reason for all of this suffering, and he sought that truth. He threw away all of his own good fortune and entered training.

For six years he did ascetic training, until at the age of thirty-six, on the morning of the eighth of December, when he saw the morning star, he awakened to the truth that he is one with the skies and earth. From then, for forty-nine years, he taught that the truth of humans is letting go of our desire and offering to everyone the hugeness of the heavens and earth. When he realized this, he saw that great truth that embraces all things. It became clear.

He saw that we don't live only from ourselves—we are embraced in the truth of the heavens and earth—and we have to know that. The Buddha taught this endlessly from his own experience: to believe in our own deepest truth and to realize that this is the purpose of our life.

For forty-nine years, he taught liberation. Then the Buddha said, "I have no more business with this world. After I am dead, my disciples will continue to teach what I have taught, and then what I have taught will always be alive. Wherever the dharma is, I am alive there, and those who see the dharma see me."

The ultimate meaning of life is to be found in prayer, I think. For me and for others who are doing training, we always read together the following sutra, which is a prayer about just this.

Dai E Zenji's Vow for Awakening

> Our only prayer is to be firm in our determination to give ourselves completely to

the Buddha's Way, so that no doubts arise, however long the road seems to be.

To be light and easy in the four parts of the body, to be strong and undismayed in body and in mind.

To be free from illness and drive out both depressed feelings and distractions.

To be free from calamity, misfortune, harmful influences and obstructions.

Not to seek the Truth outside of ourselves, so we may instantly enter the right way.

To be unattached to all thoughts, that we may reach the perfectly clear bright mind of prajna and have immediate enlightenment on the Great Matter.

Thereby we receive the transmission of the deep wisdom of the Buddhas to save all sentient beings, who suffer in the round of birth and death.

In this way we offer our gratitude for the compassion of the Buddhas and the Patriarchs.

Our further prayer is not to be extremely ill or to be suffering at the time of departure, to know its coming seven days ahead, so that we can quiet the mind to abandon the body and be unattached to all things at the last moment, wherein we return to the Original Mind in the realm of no birth and no death and merge infinitely into the whole universe, to manifest as all things in their True Nature.

And with the great wisdom of the Buddhas to awaken all beings to the Buddha Mind.

We offer this to all Buddhas and Bodhisattva-Mahasattvas of the past, present and future, in the ten quarters and to the Maha Prajna Paramita.

The dharma is the truth within our mind; it is written as the letters for flowing water and water that flows does not become ice and is always flowing. We only stop flowing because we get attached and angry at having been told something. There are big rocks and big tree roots, but to just go on around them is water flowing.

There are many difficult things in life, many kinds of roots and rocks to get caught on, but the point is to not get stopped in our mind but to be in this moment only—that is liberation. To be joyful in this very moment is liberation—to not get caught on anything at all, to be quiet and not moved around but to see that we are this mind and live in each day joyfully. This is the Buddha's eternal teaching.

Taigen Shodo Harada
Tahoma-san Sogenji Zen Monastery
September 12, 2012

Acknowledgments

I nspiration for writing this book came to me while sitting zazen. It felt like a project that needed to be done, and who was in a better position to do it than me? This kind of experience has happened to me several times: the most obvious things tend to bubble up when the mind is most quiet. So the first people I need to thank are my teacher Shodo Harada Roshi and his disciple and translator, Chisan, who have guided my practice with persistence and patience for ten years.

The idea for hospice care as both an opportunity for service to the community and as an essential component of Zen practice was being discussed by Roshi for years before I became involved with the sangha. People involved in the early discussions included Cynthia Trowbridge, Michael Lerner, Mark Albin (Yusan), Larry Zoglin (Kyosan), Jo Marie Thompson, Jim and Katrina Plato, Betsy MacGregor, Charles Terry, Ed Lorah (Gentoku), Fred Olson (Soseki), Carol Olson (Soki), Betty Brown (Myosho), Tom White, Ed Byrne (Shingen), Lee Paton, Alan Florence (Gensho), Bonnie and George Enzian, and the late Tom Kelley (Mitsuyu).

A steering committee emerged from this group, joined by Simon Leon (Shosan), Jessica Leon (Sokei), Kate Boulware, and Walt Blackford.

Ann Cutcher, MD, has been the most miraculous gift to Enso House. Her work and spirit have been the foundation for its establishment and continued operation. Commitments from Renate Krämer (MyoO) and Tim Tattu (Taigan) have enabled Enso House to flourish.

Thank you to Fredde Butterworth, Lee Compton, Jim Shelver, Keith Cunningham, Russ Ernest, Dean Petrich, Shinsan William Griswold and Shinzan Adrian Campbell for generously offering your construction skills in our remodeling projects. A special thank you to architect Ross Chapin who saw the potential in remodeling the cottage and saved it from the bulldozer.

On our board of directors, Jisai George Moseley has held our feet to the fire in the financial domain. He excels at being our "no" man. Patty Houts-Hussey who has been key to our ongoing fundraising efforts.

Thank you to all the students of Shodo Harada Roshi at Sogenji who have come to Enso House, immersed yourselves in the Fundamentals of Caregiving course, and served for months at a time as core caregivers: Hadrian Abbott, Eshin Sylvia Arkilanian, Amos Batz, Domyo Phillipe Blanche, Jikishin Linda Bland, Shinjo Jyl Brewer, Daien Lisa Brodsky, Shinzan Adrian Campbell, Genro Karen Cole, Seiwa Julie Gersten, Sojun John Godfrey, Ichigen Corey Hess, Shojun Teresa Hess, Doan Marko Kovacevic, Dairin Larry Larrick, May Lee, Sokei Jessica Leon, Jobul Tomasz Olechno, Hoetsu Joy Phillips, Kozan Piotr Roszczenko,

Genbi Gabriele Schuler, Rikke Siggaard, Taigan Tim Tattu, Peter Torma, and Ikko Arie Weezepoel, and to Jikan Regina Quitorio from Great Vow Monastery.

We have been blessed by the monks and nuns at Tahoma Zen Monastery who, while maintaining the monastery schedule of work and meditation, have also found the time to help with whatever needs arose at Enso House: Doyu Mark Albin, Jisho Varant Arslanian, Soryu Sylvia Dambrauskas, Gensho Alan Florence, Hosan, Kevin Johnson, Gentai Robert Kovacevic, Dosho Simon Leon, Sara Monial, Daigi Gregory Sellers, Myokyo Judy Skenazy, Daiko Peter Skovgaard, Blaine Venturine, and Ekei Andreas Zettl.

The secret to the ongoing vitality of Enso House is our cadre of volunteers from the South Whidbey community: Kate Boulware, Celia Bowker, Charlotte Chase, Diana Deering, Debbie Dix, Sheila Foster, Julie Gersten, Barbara Graham, Jenny Grisewood, Priya Haskins, Shirley Jantz, Diane Jhueck, Lea Kouba, Barbara Lamb, Diane Moondancer, Kathy O'Neal, Miriam Raabe, Debra Richardson, Katherine Riddle, Jo Shelver, Judy Skenazy, Janine Slabaugh, Cynthia Trenshaw, Cynthia Trowbridge, Gary Vallat, Gaea Van Breda, Claudia Walker, Theo Wells, and Sue Wright.

Thank you, Jim Rhine, for the stories of your early years living on the property.

I am grateful to the late John Stackley, who first introduced me to the connection between the property and the monastery next door.

I am especially grateful to everyone who graciously consented to being interviewed and to those who reviewed drafts of their stories and helped make them factually correct and true to spirit: Allan and Deloris Ament, Susan Chidester, Ann Cutcher, Debbie Dix, Gentoku Ed Lorah, Barbara Graham, Pam Graham, Shojun Teresa Hess, Shinkai Kurt Hoelting, Patty Houts-Hussey, Renate Krämer, Sokei Jessica Leon, Dosho Simon Leon, Michael Lerner, Wajun Brenda Loew, Betsy MacGregor, Jisai George Moseley, Hank Nelson, Soki Carol Olson, Soseki Fred Olson, Sharon Parks, James Rhine, Genbi Gabriele Schuler, Jim Shelver, Jo Shelver, Daichi Priscilla Storandt, Charles Terry, Dina Thompson, Jessica Thompson, Susan Tomic, Cynthia Trenshaw, Cynthia Trowbridge, Edie Trowbridge, Daikatsu Dennis Tucker, Gaea Van Breda, Blaine Venturine, Sue Wright and Dokyo Larry Zoglin.

Thank you to the members of our writing group, Susanne Fest, Leah Green, and Miriam Raabe, who for a period of two years have read dozens of drafts of chapters from this neophyte writer and have gently given me encouragement and constructive feedback. Thank you also to Deloris Ament, Ellen Klein, Cleo Simonett, and Gary Vallat for reviewing the work at various stages of completion. Specific content was also reviewed by Barry Wenaas, Barbara Wihlborg, Ted Stanley, and Yuho Tom Kirchner.

Some of the earliest, best, and final editing of the manuscript has been from my daughter, Allison, who has a special talent for editorial work. Thank you also to Zuiho Matthew Perez, who provided a professional edit of the manuscript.

Thank you to Paul Ginsberg of Professional Audio Laboratories, Park Ridge, New Jersey, who was able to extract audible content from an extremely poor cassette tape recording of Daichi (Chisan) Priscilla Storandt's life story recorded in 2003.

The book cover was designed by Arafa; the background photograph is from Rupac by Margerie David. Back cover layout was done by Craig Johnson. The frontispiece illustration opposite the title page is the work of Mark Morse. The author photograph on the back cover was taken by Richard Thompson. The enso calligraphy and the characters DaiKu (Great Emptiness) are the work of Shodo Harada Roshi.

Finally, I would like to thank my wife, Cynthia, for her love and affection and unfailing support for my efforts.

NOTES

[1] Translation from the French by James Evans. original translation by Denise Levertov, *Introduction to Guillevic: Selected Poems* (New Directions Books, 1969).

[2] Spike Milligan Quotes, www.spikemilligan.co.uk/spike-milligan-quotes.html, accessed Dec 6, 2012.

[3] Robert Frost, *Robert Frost's Poems* (New York: St. Martin Paperbacks, 2002).

[4] Basanta Bidari, *Kapilavastu: The World of Siddhartha* (Kathmandu: Hill Side Press, 2007).

[5] Philip Kapleau, *The Three Pillars of Zen* (New York: Anchor Books, 1965).

[6] Masaoka Shiki, quoted by Shodo Harada Roshi, Feb 26, 2010.

[7] From the video documentary, *The Man on Cloud Mountain*, Michael Yeager, (Issaquah, WA: KnowledgePath Communications, 1992).

[8] Shodo Harada, *How to do Zazen* (Kyoto, Japan: the Institute for Zen Studies, 2010).

[9] Ekai Kawaguchi, *Three Years in Tibet* (Delhi: Book Faith India, 1995).

[10] Fred and Carol Olson, letter to *Whidbey Island Friends of One Drop Zen Center*, January 28, 1996.

[11] The Buddha, *Diamond Sutra*.

[12] Carl Sagan, *Pale Blue Dot: A Vision of the Human Future in Space* (New York: Random House, 1994), p9.

[13] The Dalai Lama Tenzin Gyatoso, Nicholas Vreeland, ed., *An Open Heart: Practicing Compassion in Everyday Life* (New York: Little, Brown and Company, 2001).

[14] Carlos Castaneda, *The Teachings of Don Juan: A Yaqui Way of Knowledge* (Berkeley: University of California Press, 1968).

[15] Bernard Leach, *A Potter's Book* (London: Faber & Faber, 1988).

[16] Frank Ostaseski, *Five Precepts as Companions on the Journey to Accompany the Dying* (Alaya Institute, PO Box 2710, Sausalito, CA).

[17] The Buddha, *Vinaya Mahavagga*.

[18] Cynthia Trenshaw, *A Psalm of Deathing, a paraphrase of Psalm 139, the Bible*.

[19] Dai E Zenji's Vow for Awakening, from *Tahoma Zen Monastery sutra booklet*.

[20] Published on Psychology Today website, www.psychologytoday.com/blog/living-while-dying.

[21] Wikipedia, http://en.wikipedia.org/wiki/Oregon_Ballot_Measure_16_(1994), accessed Jan 14, 2013.

[22] Evening gatha recited at the *Zen Mountain Monastery*, Mt. Tremper, NY.

[23] Stephen Jay Gould, *The Median Isn't the Message*, Discover, June 1985.

[24] STAR Care: Samaritan Therapy And Rehabilitation.

[25] *The Book of the Craft of Dying and Other Early English Tracts Concerning Death* by Francis M. M. Compter and Robert Kastenbaum (New York: Ayer, 1977).

[26] *Bible, Revised Standard Version, 1 Corinthians 15:31.*

ABOUT THE AUTHOR

David Daiku Trowbridge has been able to pursue dual passions of scientific inquiry and spiritual quest. His affinity for the natural sciences led him to academic training in physics. Then his life took a fateful turn while teaching at a village school in Nepal, in the cradle of Buddhism. Becoming a student of Zen teacher, Shodo Harada Roshi, he took the precepts in a lay ordination ceremony. The expression of his practice involved joining with others to establish Enso House, a home for end-of-life care. He and his wife, Cynthia, live on Whidbey Island, where he is engaged in astronomy, writing, and contemplation.

Other books from Abiding Nowhere Press:

Bite into the Day: One Day at a Time, a book of poetry by Miriam Sonn Raabe

In Awe of Being Human: A Doctor's Stories from the Edge of Life and Death, by Betsy MacGregor, M.D.

Abiding Nowhere Press
www.abidingnowhere.com